JACK MITCHELL

Hug Your Customers

Love the Results

PENGUIN BOOKS

PENGUIN BOOKS

Published by the Penguin Group

Penguin Books Ltd, 80 Strand, London WC2R 0RL, England
Penguin Putnam Inc., 375 Hudson Street, New York, New York 10014, USA
Penguin Books Australia Ltd, 250 Camberwell Road, Camberwell, Victoria 3124, Australia
Penguin Books Canada Ltd, 10 Alcorn Avenue, Toronto, Ontario, Canada M4V 3B2
Penguin Books India (P) Ltd, 11 Community Centre, Panchsheel Park, New Delhi – 110 017, India
Penguin Books (NZ) Ltd, Cnr Rosedale and Airborne Roads, Albany, Auckland, New Zealand
Penguin Books (South Africa) (Pty) Ltd, 24 Sturdee Avenue, Rosebank 2196, South Africa

Penguin Books Ltd, Registered Offices: 80 Strand, London WC2R 0RL, England

www.penguin.com

Published in the United States of America by Hyperion Books 2003
Published in Great Britain in Penguin Books 2003
4

Printed in England by Clays Ltd, St Ives plc

TO BILL MITCHELL:

For all that you are—brother, husband,
father, friend.

For all your courage to face life on life's
terms.

For your special brand of leadership.

For your being my partner in building on
the values of our parents and the business
they created.

For the fun, fulfillment, and the joy of
together passing the torch and equity
to our sons.

Contents

PART TWO: From Three Suits to Three Thousand

Evolving a Hugging Organization

Acknowledgments

Nobody writes a book without a great deal of help, and I'm no exception. Dozens of relatives, associates, friends, customers, and huggers of one sort or another are due my heartfelt thanks and a big hug for their generous assistance and support.

Linda Mitchell, my wife, continues to be the love of my life. My deepest gratitude goes to her. No words can adequately express the feelings I have for her. She has done so very, very much for me and our family and given up so much of herself for others, each and every day. She gave up a potential career in science after graduating Phi Beta Kappa in physics to put me through graduate school. She balanced beautifully raising our sons and working in her family retail business. Later, she joined me in our family business, leading the women's department. We would not have a women's business today without her. And more than anyone else in my life, she has challenged me on every detail and made me reach and grow both personally and professionally. Thank you, darling.

I would never have had the success I've had without Bill, my brother, whose wisdom and unmatched hugging abilities shine every day in our stores and on every page of this book. Linda is my partner for life and for our family. Bill has been my partner in business for over thirty-three years, and I am sure will be until we exit. Clearly, we have different personalities and skill sets, and for sure we've had a few differences and challenges, but we have always had unconditional love, respect, and acceptance of each other. This book couldn't have been written without his immeasurable contribution.

I can never sufficiently thank our father, the original hugger, Ed Mitchell. Dad has always been a dreamer. I believe one of the main reasons he has lived so long—ninety-eight as we speak—is that he is always thinking about tomorrow or next year or the year after that. Probably Dad gave me the idea of visualization and forward thinking, just as Mom, God rest her soul, gave me the power to execute and the drive to excel to be the best. As a youngster, I remember her helping me every morning prepare for every test, and in high school she knew every play I called as a quarterback on the football field. She was, literally, my Monday-morning quarterback. Not second-guessing me, but encouraging me to think how I could have called plays or how I might execute them better for the next game. In addition to being grateful to them for founding Ed Mitchell Inc., I am thankful for Dad's vision and Mom's execution. My parents established our Golden Principle of everyone being on the floor and everyone treating the customers the way you would want to be treated if you were a customer—as guests in our home.

I owe particular gratitude to our four sons, Russell, Bob, Todd, and Andrew. I love and like them all as individuals. They are all very bright, well-educated, fun young men to be with, and of course to work with. I am thankful to them for their insightful advice, suggestions, and encouragement in the writing of this book. And I want to thank Russell for coming up with the title for this book. The four of them are quite a team. Somehow it seems natural, for example, that when Bob starts a sentence, Todd and Andrew add to it, and Russell ends it.

I am also grateful to Bill's three sons, Scott, Chris, and Tyler. Scott is just a delight to have as part of our family business team. He is always up, always enthusiastic, and was born wanting to improve and grow. Chris and Tyler work outside the business, but I'm keeping my fingers crossed that if they want to, and when there are real positions for them, they will join us. I deeply appreciate their support of this project.

A special thank-you to Sue Mitchell for her support of Bill, her willingness to ask the questions that needed to be asked at times when we weren't always ready to answer them, and for raising three sons who have grown up to be fine men.

A final family hug to Muriel Mitchell, Dad's new wife, who has given him a wonderful second lease on life. I love her, especially for all she's done for Dad.

A tremendous hug goes to Pamela Miles, my invaluable assistant, for her tireless work, her positive inner game, and her suggestions on behalf of this book. Without her, I'd still be dreaming about writing it.

And of course I'm indebted to our talented advisory board, for all of their hugs over the years to help us grow our business. Special thanks to Ray Rizzo, who gave me the extra nudge to go for it and write *Hug Your Customers*. To David Bork, our family business consultant, and Bob Shullman—president of the Shullman Research Group—an expert on obtaining meaningful customer feedback and improving customer service, a hundred hugs.

Big hugs, as well, to all the extraordinary associates at Mitchells and Richards (and I have listed each one of them in the appendix), for sharing their stories about hugging and living the culture of this book every day. Lots of hugs, also, to our wonderful vendors and suppliers, for being part of our family and for all they've done for us.

Many thanks and hugs to Mary Ellen O'Neill, my editor. She asked me to take a path that resulted in a much better and more readable book. And to Will Schwalbe, who believed in our hugging philosophy from the start, plus all my new friends at Hyperion. Thank you for your invaluable input and support.

I also want to extend my appreciation to Jacques de Spoelberch, my agent, for his enthusiasm and wise advice.

Finally, words cannot express my thanks to Sonny Kleinfield, my collaborator. In my eyes, Sonny is the Tiger Woods, the Michael Jordan of the literary world. Sonny has all the shots, and he made them with grace, speed, finesse, and passion throughout this entire new game for me called "book." Sonny kept my focus, articulated so well my ideas and my story, and captured and retained my voice. As dependable and reliable as Cal Ripken, Sonny was always there for me. He's very special—and he's a great hugger.

And obviously, the center of the universe for our business: To all you wonderful customers and clients, thank you, thank you, hug, hug, hug. Many of you have shared with me your stories and valuable feedback. I have never, ever forgotten that without you to hug, we would have no business.

Doesn't Everyone?

It's funny how an offhand comment at the right moment can end up crystallizing a lifetime's worth of learning. That's sort of what happened to me.

I run Mitchells/Richards, a profitable high-end clothing business in Connecticut that was founded in 1958. Today we do over $65 million in sales. A few years ago, I was invited to be a panelist at a conference that Fairchild Publications sponsored for chief executive officers in our apparel industry. The conference was held at a resort in the pleasantly named city of Carefree, Arizona. Not many of the attendees, however, were feeling especially carefree. There had been almost relentless bashing of the retail industry, and it was getting everyone down. Department stores were struggling mightily against discounters, dot comers were going to change the retail world, and people were complaining that customer service was truly dismal. The topic of the panel discussion I was on pretty much summed up the somber mood: "Apparel's Black Hole."

But it didn't sum up my mood. It's a rare day that you'll find me anything but ebullient. It's just the way I'm built. Glasses are never half empty to my eye; they're five-eighths full. Many times, they're full or overflowing. Even before the panel members were introduced, one of the keynote speakers and organizers of the event, in remarking on the decline in customer service, said that he doubted many of the several hundred executives in attendance even knew who their top one hundred customers were. He asked for a show of hands: Who knew their top hundred customers? My hand shot up. When I looked around, I couldn't see anyone else with a hand raised.

I was actually a little embarrassed to have my hand waving in the air, but mainly taken aback that no one else knew such basic and valuable information about their business. When I'm bored at home, rather than reading a book, I often punch the button on my computer and put in parameters to pull up our top one hundred or top one thousand customers, men and women, and I study them like I was studying vocabulary words for the SATs. The names go into one of the attic rooms of my brain and lodge there. As I once knew all the stats on Joe DiMaggio and Mickey Mantle, I now try to know all the stats on my top thousand customers. Because that's the game: *knowing the customer*.

Once the panelists were introduced, we were each allotted seven minutes to say something insightful on the topic of "the black hole." My take was quite a bit different from the others. The first thing I said was that I viewed retailing today not as a black hole but as a volcano. I saw it as a combination of energy, light, heat, and good things to come from the explosion. The trick was having the proper approach.

I mentioned how astonished I was that my peers didn't know their top hundred customers. I said—hopefully without sounding pompous—"I know my top one thousand customers." I told how at Mitchells everyone from the sales associate to the tailor to the delivery person concentrated on the customer, and in doing so we got remarkable results. I was thinking of all the customers we have that spend $5,000 a year, year after year, at our stores, about the customers that spend $20,000 a year and those that spend $100,000. We even have a few that spend $250,000. That's right, $250,000 a year on clothes at our stores. I was thinking about how we embrace every customer with a friendly greeting and a smile. I thought about the two dozen sales associates who write at least $1 million a year in business. It used to be unheard-of for anyone to do $1 million, but now we expect that the first year someone joins us. We even have five associates who write $2 million, and one who writes an unthinkable $3 million—in a town of 28,000 people! That's a lot of suits and dresses, and we sell them one at a time. One customer at a time.

I went on to relate some of the stories about the elaborate and at times adventuresome extents we go to in order to exceed the expectations of our customers. Once I had exhausted my seven minutes, I was really pumped. I get that way when I talk about our business. I returned to my table, and one of my tablemates, thinking over my anecdotes, smiled at me and said, "Oh, sure, Jack. The next thing you're going to tell us is that you and your sales associates actually hug your customers."

I looked at him and, without blinking, replied, "Sure. Doesn't everyone?"

And that's when it became crystal clear in my mind. Everyone didn't do what we did, and what we did was hug our customers. We were a bunch of huggers. In some instances, we *physically* hug the customers—I've seen sales associates actually give customers a bear hug and then dance with them around the floor—but we mainly metaphorically hug them by showering them with attention in a way that every business ought to but doesn't. From then on, I began referring to how we treat customers at Mitchells/Richards as "hugging"—first to myself, then to the family and associates—and it seemed to fit, like a great suit. Everything else we do—like what I call "The Big Secret" and "The Formula" and "Game Day"—springs from this simple but essential practice. Hugging, in my mind, implies passion, and without passion and commitment, customer service can never be extraordinary. People have said to me, "Jack, you are obsessed with extraordinary customer service!"

This book is about one particular family's philosophy of selling. For three generations, my family has been dressing men and women in Fairfield and Westchester Counties, where a high concentration of top executives live and increasingly work. Our stores are less than an hour by train from New York's Grand Central Station, but we are told we're a world apart in terms of the care, time, and attention we devote to each and every customer. My parents started the business in 1958 in a former plumbing supply store with a bare-bones inventory of three suits and all the free coffee you could drink. My mother would make coffee for customers in the same pot she used to make breakfast at home, so she made sure to bring the pot home with her at the end of the day for a good scrubbing. That first year, they did $50,000 worth of sales and were thrilled.

Nowadays, we have two stores in Connecticut, Mitchells and Richards. We do in excess of $65 million a year, and we are all thrilled to be selling suits and dresses one at a time and hugging customers. We achieve this volume in Westport, a town of just 28,000 people, and in nearby Greenwich, which has about 60,000. Roughly every other household is a customer in our system, because at some point we gave them a very pleasant and memorable shopping experience—a hug or two that made them come back for more. We've been told by others that we're one of the most successful—if not *the* most successful— high-end clothing businesses of our size in the country, and maybe in the world. It's not because of our product, it's not because of our prices—other stores have great product at the same prices—it's because of how we personally treat customers.

I don't think it's an overstatement to say that more than any other retailer of our size, we clothe corporate America. Our customers include the chief executives, presidents, owners, chief financial officers, division managers, and entrepreneurs of many of the companies that are household names: GE, IBM, Verizon, Coke, Pepsi, JP Morgan Chase, Gillette, Merrill Lynch, Lehman Brothers, American Skandia, Xerox, and many more. I counted it up once and found out that more than five hundred chief executives and presidents are our customers, along with literally thousands of executives and men and women who work for their firms. We outfit quite a few film luminaries and sports stars too—in other words, people who are successful and who care how they look. They know that clothes are extraordinarily powerful in the business world. While clothes don't really "make the woman or man," they often make a huge difference in their careers. And I'm proud to say our customers also include local firefighters and police officers who I went to school with, who like to look great, too.

That may sound well and good, but why should you care how we sell? Because I firmly believe that our philosophy is in no way restricted to suits and dresses, and that's why I wanted to write a book. In addition, so many loyal customers and friends have urged me to try to share our story to help all businesses do a better job of satisfying their clientele at a time when disillusioned customers are howling to be treated better.

Like so many people, I find myself continually frustrated at the passionless customer service I encounter every day. Not long ago, I went to my regular supermarket, where I go week after week, looking for a turkey, and they said they had none. How can you run out of turkeys? And the store managers didn't offer to find me one or direct me somewhere else, or even simply apologize for not having any. Their attitude was, tough luck. For probably fifteen years, my family and I bought something like two dozen Chevys at the local Chevy dealer, and yet in all that time the salesman never once called to see how the cars were running or to point out that I was about due to look at a new car. Not a peep. Once the car was off the lot, I was forgotten as a customer.

Rare are the times when the opposite happens. But when it does, I'm bowled over. Years ago, when IBM was trying to sell us computers, I was chatting with the salesman and happened to mention I needed to go up to New Hampshire to see one of my sons in a sports event. He said, "Hey, I recently got my pilot's license. I'll fly you up. Let's go." I thought, "Wow!"

And that's how the IBM relationship began. A hug in a small airplane.

That's what Mitchells is about: making people say, "Wow!" I'd like to see that happen in every business. For there's no doubt in my mind that our philosophy can readily be applied to selling just about anything—macaroni, aircraft engines, carpets, stocks and bonds, insurance, or beanbags. The management theory we use to run Mitchells will work in any business that has customers, and I can't think of too many that don't.

Our philosophy is built on a lifetime of being on the floor selling clothes. I still try to be on the floor every day, a tape measure draped around my neck, finding someone's size, directing a customer to the proper department. But while I've injected my ideas here and there, my job has been more of a collator and facilitator of great ideas. Because our philosophy of selling is truly a family philosophy. There are nine Mitchells in the business, including my ninety-eight-year-old father, who started it all, and every one of them has contributed something vital to how we operate. My parents, through their hard work establishing the business, formulated many of the principles that continue to this day. My brother Bill, who has always been my valued partner, has taught me endless lessons about how to sell the hugging way, and Mitchells wouldn't be the great success it's become without him. Bill's the one on the floor swapping the latest jokes, and generally acting as the smiling maître d' of Mitchells. We have seven sons between us, and while I've taught my sons and his sons a lot, they've also taught me. When I write about how we sell at Mitchells, I'm writing about a philosophy assembled from the collective ingenuity of three generations of Mitchells.

Our vision is that anyone that becomes a customer of our stores enters an enduring relationship with us. He or she instantly becomes our friend. That's our motto: "Once a customer, always a friend." It's been that way since the day the doors opened, and it will always be that way. It's clear to me that customers are thirsting for relationship-driven companies. They want to be coddled. They like it when they are smiled at. They appreciate thank-you notes. And great sellers want to work for relationship-driven companies. Those companies are more successful because relationship selling inevitably leads to high productivity and high profitability. In a relationship-driven company, it's a lot more fun to go to work in the morning. And we want to have fun.

We're successful at Mitchells, I believe, not because we recognize that relationships work. Many companies grasp that. The difficult part is getting relationships to happen. And that's where hugging comes in. Execution is everything. After all, it can be boring to sell a suit over and over again, or to sell a car or a lawn mower over and over again. But you can meet this challenge by approaching every customer as a unique challenge and opportunity. That's what I hope to show you how to do.

The way I've written the book is very much the way I talk, which is to mix big-picture business philosophy with real-life stories, and there's a dash of Mitchells history in there to boot. I've also sprinkled lists of key ideas and principles throughout the chapters, for those who like lists. Because I want to hug my readers, I've included a Hugging Study Guide at the end of each section that sums up the key points I've covered. In the appendix, you'll find a "hugging game" of sorts I call the Hugging Achievement Test (the H.A.T.). Don't worry, it's all for fun, and the results won't get sent out to any colleges.

I feel I've truly been blessed with a great family and a wonderful business I can be proud of. I love to talk, tell stories, and share, and I especially love to talk about what I know, which is selling. And hugging. So let's get started and find out how to hug.

PART ONE

Hugging 101

The Principles of Passionate Customer Service

Chapter 1

Creating a Hugging Culture

It always seems like emergencies come up when you're not ready for them, and that's exactly what happened during the escapade of the navy blue cashmere topcoat. It was a cold winter day in early February. My brother was off on a business trip. I was out of the store at an advertising meeting. A call came in to Mitchells and the challenge was immediately forwarded to me. A manager at a nearby corporation who was a client of ours had phoned from his office and desperately needed a navy blue cashmere topcoat. He was going to an important acquisition meeting in New York, and when he checked his closet, it turned out that his sons had swiped all his coats when they went off to college. The man's energy level is so high he generally doesn't wear coats. But the forecast was for cold temperatures and heavy snow, and his meetings would require him to do a fair bit of walking in New York, and so it was imperative that he have a coat in navy blue.

I called the store, only to learn that we had sold out of navy cashmere coats in size 42, the man's size. But we did have a light gray one. I alerted Domenic Condoleo, our master tailor, and told him to gather up the gray topcoat as well as some suits, sport coats, and a few accessories for the client's consideration. I'm a salesman through and through, and if I was going over there to sell him a topcoat, you can bet I was going to take along some other items too.

I promptly got in touch with our two topcoat resources, one in Philadelphia and the Hickey-Freeman facility in Rochester, New York. They both had navy cashmere topcoats in stock and promised to overnight them to the store. Then I called the client's secretary and told her Domenic and I were on our way over. When we got there, we schlepped the garment bags to the third floor. The manager jumped up from his desk, and said, "Where's my blue topcoat?" I calmly opened the garment bags and slipped the gray topcoat on him. Naturally, he immediately said, "Jack, this is gray." He was annoyed. Either he thought I hadn't listened or I was colorblind, and said so in very expletive-deleted terms.

"I know," I said. "Like you at your company, we like to turn all of our product at least three times, and we've sold all the blue ones. We're getting two in tomorrow."

"Can't wait, can't wait!" he screamed. "I'm going to see if we can get the company's helicopter ready to pick up the coats. Where are they coming from?"

"Just calm down," I said. "You can wait until tomorrow. I'll meet you in New York City." His office TV was on with the stock market news, and he noticed that the company's stock was going up, and his disposition improved. I seized the moment to move on to the suits, sport coats, and shirts we had brought along. Just as I suspected, he selected a few things, but he hadn't forgotten about the topcoat. Some people were waiting to see him, so his secretary brought in our coats so we could leave, and here's where the *hug* came. I don't know why I didn't think of this before, but it struck me that my topcoat was a navy blue cashmere from Hickey-Freeman, size 42. I said to the man, "Put this on."

It fit perfectly. He jumped up and down in glee. I said to him, "Tell you what, we'll lease my coat to you for a day or two."

He loved the idea. "Wow, Mitchells is in the leasing business, just like we are," he said.

Two days later, we delivered the man's new coat. This may strike you as a lot of effort to please a customer—literally giving him the coat off my back. But the reality is, we do it all the time, even for someone shopping with us for the first time.

That's what "Hugging 101" is all about.

Over the last forty-five years, my family has been dedicated to providing the highest level of customer service possible. We use the term *hugging* to describe our unique selling culture, and in this first part I will take you on a personal tour of our world of Mitchell hugging. I think of hugging as getting everyone on your team to sell with passion so you develop long-term loyal relationships with your customers. Those are the keys: company-wide passion and long-term relationships. This company-wide relationship-building centered around the customer is what marketing gurus call *relationship marketing*. Passion, in particular, is something I believe in wholeheartedly. I guess you could say I'm passionate about passion.

Hugging involves touching and listening to and caring about the customer, getting so close to the customer that the customer becomes more important than anything else. Over time in a hugging culture, a unique personal and professional relationship develops between the business and customer—a loyalty built on trust and, in our case, sales that fill closets with clothes customers love to wear and are right for them.

Once relationships are established with customers, they become friends. I'm not suggesting that every customer becomes a true best friend who would confide his deepest secrets or we'd invite to come along on our vacations. That would be a little strange (though some customers do in fact become that close). We mean *friend* in the sense of someone who comes to trust you and enjoys your company. The distinction is we get to know them better than a traditional customer, and they get to know us better. All by hugging.

For a hugging culture to work, everyone in the organization, from top to bottom, must embrace it. That means everyone from me to the buyers to the tailors to the credit managers to the shipping clerks. In a hugging culture, *everyone* hugs and *everyone* sells, not just the people who collect the commissions. I can't emphasize that enough.

It takes hard work to achieve a hugging culture—it doesn't happen overnight—but I'm convinced it's well worth the effort. After all, hugging is universally appealing. Everyone loves to be hugged. There's nothing controversial about it. It simply works.

Of course, it also works financially. It certainly does for us. Every month, our controller meets with us regarding the cash flow, inventory turn, and other financial paradigms that show that it works.

And one of the best things about hugging is how versatile it is. It's a business philosophy that succeeds just as well for someone selling margarine or laptops. Any company in any industry can learn to hug.

Try it. Try it before the day is over. Smile and hug. See if your customers—or daughter, or assistant—don't smile and hug you back.

Chapter 2

The New Business Landscape

Why is a hugging culture so important? It's because we believe retailing, and business in general, has undergone a fundamental shift in
thinking and behavior in the last decade, a shift that cries out for
hugging. In particular, I've noticed three critical changes in the business landscape that are embraced by successful companies.

REACTIVE → PROACTIVE

The first big change was moving from a reactive to a proactive
approach. In the 1970s and early 1980s, sales associates stood around
and waited for people to come into the store. You waited and you
reacted: "May I help you?" And we did. But that doesn't work any
longer. Now you need to be proactive. You can't stand idly twiddling
your thumbs until someone walks in the door. You have to take actions

that will bring customers through that door. In other words, you need to initiate the sale, not simply complete it.

TRANSACTIONS → RELATIONSHIPS

Years ago, everything was transaction-based. The interaction with the customer began and ended with the transaction. Say the customer bought three suits, six white shirts, and a couple of ties, one striped and one solid. You had no complaints. That was a nice sale, and you earned a nice commission. End of discussion. You had no idea what the person was going to do with those suits and shirts, and it wasn't that you didn't care, you just didn't have the mindset to ask the customer.

Today it's not enough to just make a sale. We have to ask the customer what he is using those three new suits for, and then we can decode that into what type suit, fabric, color, and model is right for him. Often we know a lot more than he does about what he should wear in the business or social setting to look and feel great. If he travels a lot, you set him up with a harder fabric. In the old days, you might have sold him a thousand-dollar suit and he packed it in a carry-on bag and the first time he put it on it was all wrinkled. Today you have to listen in order to understand the customer's needs, and that means developing a *personal* relationship with him.

Anyone can sell a dark blue suit. Anyone can sell a wheelbarrow. But that's not a relationship.

So selling has shifted from transactions to relationships. It's moved from a "May I help you?" transaction to "Is the new outfit for business or a special occasion?" You're researching need. The critical difference in making this shift is how you think about customers. I believe in staying as close as possible to the customer.

MAGIC LIST → CUSTOMER-LED
SERVICES

There's a third change that has taken place. It used to be that businesses had what I call a "magic list," an assortment of little extra services they provided all customers as an incentive to shop with them: free parking, free alterations, free coffee, and a liberal return policy. The magic list defined service. Any business could draw up its own list. We had this list, and we still have it. These things do matter. But magic lists are no longer enough. Through the relationships you develop, you must listen to your customers on an individual basis so that you know her or him, and give them additional services that are important to them.

I call these customer-led services. Some customers, for instance, because of schedule or a phobia about crowds, might want to shop during off-hours. So you open the store at night for them. Or you fit them in a private dressing room. Let me give you another example that may sound silly, but it works. Every Saturday in the summer outside Mitchells we give away hot dogs. After a while, we added kosher dogs for our Jewish clientele. A loyal customer whose first name is Carole had high cholesterol, so we got some turkey dogs for her. She showed up every Saturday to get one, and so we started calling it the Carole Dog. The Carole Dog is a customer-led service. It's a matter of being willing to deviate from the magic list and doing "one-plus."

In the hotel industry, a standard list of services gets you three or four or five stars. But have you ever stayed at a four-star hotel that you liked more than some five stars? Sure, and the reason you liked it more was because you were hugged. Perhaps the waitress remembered your favorite type of tea or coffee at breakfast without your asking. The magic list doesn't matter. What matters is passionate service and hugs.

FROM *SATISFIED* TO *EXTREMELY* SATISFIED CUSTOMERS

Add these changes together, and what you get is satisfied customers who are transformed into *extremely* satisfied customers. You move from meeting expectations to *exceeding* expectations. Carole might have expected to get a hot dog, but she never expected a Carole Dog. And the day I gave her that first Carole Dog, she gave me a hug back—actually, it was a big passionate kiss on the cheek. It felt great.

The reality is that satisfied customers simply aren't enough anymore to make a prosperous business. They aren't really loyal and will readily defect at the slightest prompt. **Only extremely satisfied customers are genuinely loyal.**

OLD		NEW
Reactive	→	Proactive
Transactions	→	Relationships
"Magic" List	→	Customer-Led Services
Satisfied Customers	→	Very Satisfied Customers
Very Satisfied Customers	→	Extremely Satisfied Customers
Meet Expectations	→	Exceed Expectations

Chapter 3

The Customer-Centric Organization

The way we've adapted to these powerful changes in the business world at Mitchells is by creating a customer-centric organization rather than a product- or price-centric organization. We feel customer-centric organizations are the best huggers. By *customer-centric*, I mean the customer is the center of the universe. Everything revolves around the customer. Everyone says the customer is important, but in most businesses, actions speak otherwise. The power of a customer-centric philosophy comes from dedicating the entire organization and its focus to the customer. You cannot become customer-centric until *all* parts of the organization passionately embrace the customer.

It's obvious to me that many leading businesses, whether they sell clothes or cornbread, are all about product. If they're in the clothing business like us, they're interested in whether it's a so-called Super 100 wool fabric or a Super 180. Is it handmade or machine-made? Is it light gray or olive? Two- or three-button? Short or long shirt?

At Mitchells, clothes are not our priority. It's not the first thing we think of, nor the last. Don't get me wrong. We like fabulous product, and we search the world to get it, but we're all about customers.

Now that may sound amazing. A clothing store that isn't about clothes? But it's true. And if we were a restaurant, we wouldn't be about food. If we were an electronics store, we wouldn't be about DVD players. Businesses have lost sight of the idea that customers, not product, are the most important priority. Most companies think all you have to do is have plenty of great product and the right value and customers will descend like locusts on their stores. Many stores have those things. You can buy a great blue blazer or black skirt anywhere. You can buy a great flat-screen TV at any electronics store. You can get a great sofa at a lot of furniture stores. It's how you treat customers that determines your long-term success. To prosper today, you have to think *customer* before concepts like *return on investment* and *margins*. Far too many business managers have no idea who their customers are, or what their customers want, or what their perceptions are, and haven't a clue as to how to find out.

If you become customer-centric, it means you personalize the relationship between the seller and the buyer. It means your entire company listens and learns from your customers. It means you give customers what they want rather than what you want to sell them. It means you know customers' preferences better than they do, and can predict what they want.

I'm always saying to our associates, know more about your customers than your merchandise. In my business, we have what's called an SKU, a stock-keeping unit. It uniquely defines an item. It could designate the style, size, and color of a suit or dress. At Mitchells/Richards, we like to say we SKU our customers (when I tell people this, I make sure I spell it out, "S-K-U," so they don't think I mean "screw our customers"). We're trying to measure and understand our customers in every possible way. We have over 115,000 customers in our database, and by listening and learning over the years we get to know a great deal about every one of them.

To create hugging relationships, it's essential to have people with long tenure, and we pride ourselves on that. Sometimes it takes more time than you would like for an associate to really get it, but when they do, it becomes natural, and that's why tenured associates are so productive. We've been told our tenure is much better than most of the other great stores. Our store managers, Tom Maleri and Jeff Kozak, average seventeen years. Our head tailors average thirty years of service. You build great relationships if you work at it for thirty years. When I have conversations with peers, they constantly mention how high their turnover is. From time to time, they do cite very long term associates, but it's usually in the context of people who are old and tired whom they would like to take early retirement.

Once you've built a customer-centric organization, you'll find that customer loyalty builds over time, and with it, profitability. The true key to long-term profitability is strong and enduring relationships between the customers and the seller. When you have strong relationships, customers will do more of their buying from you. They'll refer other customers. They'll communicate with you better and tell you what they like and what they don't like, in turn making your business more efficient and effective. Your best customers are the ones who most want you to do well, so it makes sense to learn from them. And loyal customers will be more forgiving if you do something wrong, and return fewer items because you know their sizes, and their likes and dislikes.

In a customer-centric organization, everyone automatically thinks of the customer before anything else. Let me offer a little story that illustrates this.

Ray Rizzo is a great customer, and his father was a real character, and not the easiest man in the world to fit. He had a tendency to undergo wide weight fluctuations, and he often was on the short and portly side, not your standard size. Some years ago, Ray's dad was living in New Orleans and he had driven up to Connecticut to visit Ray for Christmas. The Rizzo clan was going out on Christmas Eve to a friend's home, and Ray's dad had forgotten to bring along anything suitable to wear. He didn't have a sport coat or a good pair of pants—nothing. So Ray told him, "Let's go to Mitchells."

When they got to the store, it was already four o'clock. They were going out at six. Needless to say, things were a little tight. Ray spotted me and bounded over and said, "Jack, we've got a problem." He explained the situation and I told him, "Fine, let's measure your dad." We did a measurement and it was looking grim. He was a 53 short jacket and a 48 regular waist. No store anywhere in the world would have had something on the rack that would fit those dimensions, or even come close to fitting them, and here it was, Christmas Eve. Where was Santa Claus when you really needed him?

So I went to Ray and I said, "Oh, man, he is a real portly short size, and we don't stock those sizes. Your dad has a challenging body." We both chuckled. Then I said, "But let's talk to Domenic, our head tailor, and see what we can do." So I sat Ray and his dad down, gave them something to drink, and Dom got cracking. Now Dom already knew Ray and his dad, because everyone in our organization interacts with the customer. Because Dom knew them, he cared about them. Because he cared about them, what mattered wasn't that it was almost closing time and it was Christmas Eve. What mattered was that Ray's dad needed some clothes—and fast.

And so Dom rounded up the biggest jacket and biggest pair of pants he could find. In about an hour's time, he and his team in the tailor's shop had transformed them into an outfit that fit Ray's dad perfectly. He looked like a million bucks and felt the same. Hug, hug, as he thanked Dom and me more than a hundred times.

I remember driving home that Christmas Eve feeling so proud of Domenic that he went the extra yard. Just as important, I was proud that our family had been successful in establishing an environment where Domenic created the miracle without the owner telling him he had to do so.

Chapter 4

The Golden Principle

You can't truly become customer-centric unless the entire organization is integrated so that everyone touches the customers, and so you have to ensure and enable that that happens. We have very few rules in our organization, because I hate rules. I hated them as a kid, I hated them in college, and I still hate them. A rules-based company has a tough time hugging. So we have principles, not rules, and our Golden Principle, essential to a hugging culture, is that everyone, at some point, works on the floor. Of course that includes Bill and me. It starts at the top. And if Dad shows up, even at ninety-eight the odds are he'll get out on the floor and try to sell something or schmooze with the customers as he circles the store, and sometimes they actually follow him like he's the grand pied piper.

The reason I'm on the floor every day for at least a period of time and all day on Saturdays and busy days, with a tape measure around my neck, is to send the message that no one is so high up in the organization that they are above waiting on customers. To customers and associates, it shows that you're ready for business. You have to deliver the message from the top. I consider it an honor, a privilege, and a pleasure to wait on customers. Relationship selling is based on owners or senior management on the floor. Some businesses don't have an actual selling floor like we do (the telephone is the floor in the brokerage business, and I suppose the customer's living room is the floor in the life insurance business), but what I mean is that everyone must be able to interact with the customer.

The reason I want everyone on the selling floor at some point is that's where it's easiest to see, touch, and feel real live customers. That's why we don't have a warehouse where there's shipping and receiving. It's inside both of the stores. The shipping people take the time and the care to wrap and package clothing that is being sent out because they see the customers upstairs and get to know them. If you know someone by name, then that motivates you to make sure that when the customer opens his garment it's pressed properly and so he feels hugged. That's why the tailor shops are on the premises, so I can bring the customers into the shop and introduce them to what we call the United Nations, because we've got tailors from a dozen different countries altering the clothes. They meet the customers, and so they take pride when they sew that garment to take a meeting at the White House or for the wedding of a customer's only daughter.

Our principle of everyone on the floor is why we don't have an outside advertising agency. Everything is done out of a little office in our store. The managers and sales associates take the time to personalize almost every single piece of marketing: "Hi Allison, hope you're enjoying the summer. This new suit would look great on you." Or,

"Hi, Debbie, hope the trip went well, we've got a great new sweater that was made for you." The advertising department is on the floor, and knows the customer. That way the advertising people know that the sales associates hug differently from one customer to the next and therefore how critical each little personal note is that they put on each mailing to develop long-term loyal relationships.

And let's not forget the buyers, perhaps the most important huggers outside of the sales associates. I doubt there's another business in the country that has buyers on the floor as often as we do, selling, listening, and learning about what the customers want. Most buyers never see the floor, let alone a customer. Real live people.

To me, it's common sense that the buyers ought to be on the floor. After all, they're the ones going out and choosing the products for these customers. How can they choose appropriate product if they never interact with the customers? When Phyllis Bershaw, our Number 1 seller, uses Linda Mitchell, my wife and our women's buyer, as a resource by saying to her, "Help me find a special dress for Marianne for a big occasion," Linda actually knows Marianne and what would best suit her. And when she's in New York, Paris, or Milan buying the next season's fashion collections, she is thinking Marianne as the models waltz down the runways. That's a big hug. Or when Bob Mitchell introduces a new collection to both the men's and women's departments, it's not because he has this otherworldly hunch. It's because he knows we have clients who would delight in these very luxurious and expensive clothes picked out with them in mind. That's a hug.

Even our finance people visit the floor. Loyal customers translate into superior profit, and yet most people in finance have never met a loyal customer, don't know why they're loyal, and don't even realize they're the source of all the beans they're counting. Yet chief financial officers at a great many businesses routinely make broad decisions that undermine a company's ability to deliver hugs.

As all of this suggests, one of the ways you can tell if your company is customer-centric is to look at where the offices are. Where is the CEO's office, the tailor shop, the buyers' and accounting offices? They should be in the store, not at a distribution center, or you lose the personal interaction between the associates and the customers.

By having everyone on the floor, everyone sees the need to hug, and that triggers additional hugs. It's a hug when we fly in the senior fitter from Italy to fit one of our top customers. It's a hug when the buyers combine with marketing to put on a trunk show. It's a hug when we hold a golf outing, where we invite all of our major manufacturers and designers, plus our top customers. The customers love the hugging experience of playing golf with celebrated manufacturers and designers. It's a hug when we take over a local restaurant and invite our top customers for an evening of thanks and to hear journalist Carl Bernstein speak.

And when I say "everyone on the floor," I don't mean strictly the selling floor, but wherever our customers happen to be. Season after season, as we've done for forty years, all of us wake up early in the morning and go to the railroad stations in Westport, Greens Farms, Wilton, Fairfield, Greenwich, and Rye, and we give away newspapers and coffee from six in the morning until eight. It's a hug, a big one. People look at us and say, "What are you doing?" And we tell them, "We're here to say, 'Free *New York Times* and coffee, and thank you.'" And then, while they're sitting on the train, they open up their newspapers and our spring or fall promotional piece falls into their laps and they can't help but look at it. And smile. Now that's a hug.

Chapter 5

Hugging Is a Mindset

The very word "hugging" may suggest we're advocating all sorts of fuzzy, touchy-feely type of stuff. We're not, though warmth is a big part of our business. I define hugging as a mindset more than a physical act. It's a way of thinking about customers. To us, hugging is a softer word for passion and relationships. It's a way of getting close to your customers and truly understanding them. I like to say, You listen, you learn, you hug.

In the simplest sense, a hug is anything that exceeds a customer's expectations. It can be as commonplace as a smile or eye contact. It could be a firm handshake. It could be speeding up the tailoring process for a new customer, who wouldn't be expecting expedited service. It could be remembering a customer's name, even though it's only the second time you've seen him, and the first time was two years ago. It could be asking about the customer's children, and knowing their names and ages, even though there are five of them. It's remembering where they work. When the new chief financial officer of a big company came in and I greeted him by congratulating him that his company's stock rose five dollars the previous day, he was blown away. That's a hug.

Everyone in our company hugs differently, and that's the way it should be. Some people are comfortable giving a bear hug. Others recoil at anything too physical. That's fine. Those people like to shake hands, or give a high five, or look you in the eye, or send personal notes. You adopt the hug that works for you and your customer.

Once, as an exercise, I sat down and drew up a list of different hugs, and I got to thirty-three before I started to get a cramp in my hand. Some of the ones I wrote down were: Offer someone a beverage or snack, carry their bags to the car, send a birthday card, send an anniversary card, remember names, sew on a button, press pants, call when you say you will, send flowers on a holiday, send flowers after a big sale, call and invite to lunch at the store, make reservations for someone at an exclusive restaurant, get tickets to a ball game or the theater, open the store after hours for private appointments, have a liberal return policy that allows you to give money back with a smile, call another store to get something you don't have, show product knowledge, smile, resolve credit issues instantly, give a firm handshake, look a customer in the eyes as a friend who cares, exchange business cards, telephone someone who's sick to show you care, send an e-mail (especially to people who travel internationally), listen. A woman once brought in a dress she had bought at Bergdorf's that needed to be altered in a hurry. We did it for her. That's a hug. Almost every Saturday night, I guarantee it, someone will come in, if not two or three, and there's some formal event in town, and he wants someone to tie his bow tie. In Westport, that would be Bruce, our designated bow tier extraordinaire. In Greenwich, it's my nephew Scott, who recently responded to an SOS and raced over to tie an entire wedding party at their home twenty minutes before the ceremony. That's a hug.

One of the best hugs of all is a letter of thanks, and it's a big hug if it's handwritten and a very big hug if you write an additional handwritten note on the side of a typed letter. This especially matters with someone we've just met. The first-time customer is extremely important, because first impressions are so powerful. You never get them back. We go out of our way to start off on the right foot. In a good year, we open up thousands of new customer accounts at both stores. Every time we get a new customer, a letter is generated from our computer that I sign. It more or less says, "I hope you enjoyed shopping at Richards and that Frank Gallagi provided you with everything you needed. Your Zegna suit will be ready on Tuesday and will look terrific with your Armani tie."

The notes weren't my idea, but I like to take good ideas I hear about in other businesses and adapt them to ours. I learned about this concept from Tauck World Discovery, an international tour business based in Westport. Every time a trip is completed, the tour leader circulates a questionnaire among the participants. From that questionnaire, a personal letter is derived that goes out to the participants. Many people know it's computer-generated, but it is signed one note at a time and it has a big impact.

A while ago, Linda, my wife, bought something at Bergdorf's. They sent her a form letter, printed but signed in script, from the president. She was impressed, and it takes a lot to impress her. She's a very savvy and sophisticated woman. Why was she impressed? She said because for spending just a few hundred dollars she got a letter. In my judgment, it got her attention because the letter came from Number One. There is a certain instinctual respect for the power in the position of Number One. More about that later. So even if someone came in and bought nothing other than a handbag on sale, she gets a letter from me. I'll bet she comes back and buys a lot more on the next visit.

A hug can be a thoughtful remedy for an annoyance. When the Postal Service raised the price of a stamp to 37 cents from 34 cents, my first thought was, "Oh, great, now I've got to stand in line to get 3-cent stamps so I can use that mound of 34-cent stamps I bought so I wouldn't have to wait in line for a long time." I hate waiting in lines, especially at a government agency. But who doesn't? So I sent out a personal note to five hundred of our good customers, thinking they might be in the same boat, and included some 3-cent stamps. "You know you are the focus of our business," I wrote. "In an effort to make your life less hectic, I have enclosed a handful of 3-cent stamps." It was a hug out of nowhere, and they loved it.

Sometimes, a hug is a means to solve a very particular problem. Frank Gallagi has been a sales associate at Richards for thirty-eight years, and he's a born hugger. There's no doubt in my mind, he came out of the womb ready to hug. Many years ago, Matt Lauer, the *Today* show host, used to work as a sales associate at Richards. Matt happens to be slightly colorblind, which can be problematic when a customer wants you to match shirts and ties with suits. Matt loves to tell his story of how Frank and he devised a system of signals that Frank would flash Matt when he was with a customer to let him know what went with what and to keep him from suggesting a brown shirt with a dark blue suit. A lasting friendship was born.

Matt is now a client of Frank's, and naturally he is still a friend. With Matt's colorblindness, it can get a little dicey trying to get dressed for the show at 4:30 in the morning. Enter Frank and his camera. For years, Frank has maintained a clothes book for Matt and many of his other clients. Matt has great style and flair, but he still asks Frank's advice when he buys new clothes. Frank snaps pictures of them and then he arranges the pictures in a book that shows what goes together. By relying on these books, Matt never misses on color and he always looks impeccable. There are also sections devoted to what to wear for special occasions, outings, anything Matt might have to do that involves clothing. Frank began doing this with one of those Polaroid instant cameras, graduated to a 35 mm, and now works with a digital camera. I noticed that *Esquire* and other national magazines recently named Matt as one of their ten best-dressed men. We are extremely proud, and we couldn't be happier that he gets his clothes from us.

I could go on and on, and I'm sure you can think up your own ideas in your own businesses that aren't on this list.

Once you've worked long enough in a hugging culture and acquired that hugging mindset, nothing seems impossible. For instance, Mitchells delivers hundreds of packages to friends throughout Connecticut. So what, right? Many businesses deliver.

But how many businesses, when the circumstances demand it, will dig out their passports and make an international delivery?

Years ago, my brother Bill got a call from a local family that shopped at Mitchells. Their son was studying in Tokyo, and tragically, his roommate had been killed in a car accident. The son needed to go to his funeral the next day, and he didn't have anything suitable to wear. Being in college, he had plenty of jeans and T-shirts, but his one blue suit was hanging in his closet in Westport. He was an odd size, a 39 Long, and there was no way he could quickly find a substitute in Tokyo. Was there any way we could get his suit to him in time?

This was a challenge, and it didn't even involve a new sale. But Bill got on the phone and reached a retired American Airlines pilot he knew in Florida. He explained the situation and the pilot said he would make some calls. A little later, Bill heard back from him: No luck. Bill took a deep breath and called over to one of the major corporations based in Connecticut, since many of the top executives shopped at our store. In short order, the executive secretary reported back to Bill that an executive was leaving to go to Singapore on the corporate jet and could take the suit. Bill knew that while Singapore was closer to Tokyo than Westport, it was still not Tokyo. The executive secretary said, "Don't worry. The plane has to go on to Japan." The plane dropped the executive off in Singapore, took the suit to Tokyo, where it was picked up by the college student, and then returned to Singapore to retrieve the executive. Even by our standards, that's a monumental hug.

When you acquire the hugging mindset, you'll naturally come up with all sorts of passionate ways to care for your customers.

Chapter 6

Everyone in the Kitchen

The very atmosphere of our stores is a major hug in itself. Every year, I reread Stanley Marcus's book *Minding the Store*, because Stanley was a legendary retailer and Neiman Marcus is a great store. One of the things I've always liked about the book is how Stanley speaks of Neiman Marcus as a home, because that's the way Mom and Dad always talked about our store, and it's the way I've continued to speak about it. When someone comes into Mitchells or Richards, we welcome them as if we are welcoming a guest into our home. We welcome them as a friend.

And since the idea is we're greeting a friend, I put a firm emphasis on and encourage all associates to remember and use first names. I've long been a big believer in the power of first names. You don't welcome a friend at your front door as "Mr. Jenkins" or "Mrs. Rapoport." You say, "Hi, Holman" or "Hi, Janet." And if someone goes by a nickname, you'd better know it. Imagine if someone called me John, my given name, instead of Jack. That wouldn't be a hug, it would be a slap. Since you're greeting a friend, you ask them if they'd like a cup of coffee. Or would the kids like a balloon?

I even refer to sections of our stores as if they were rooms in our home. I call the central area where the checkout is the "kitchen," because that's where most of the activity takes place, just like in a home. It's the cozy area people feel comfortable in. You know how, when you have dinner guests over, you're always trying to shoo them into the living room, but they insist on hanging out in the kitchen. It's the same way in our store. People congregate there, and that's where the coffee bar is, as well as the television. The coffeepot has always been on at Mitchells. It's one of our signature ways of welcoming you, because coffee reflects hospitality. Only now we don't just offer you coffee. We put out trays of other beverages too. And at Mitchells we offer free M&M's and muffins and bagels. Isn't that what you do when friends come to your home? How many stores have you been in where there are signs on the entrance doors, "No food or beverages allowed in the store." You'll never see a sign like that at Mitchells or Richards. After all, we're serving you food and beverages.

And—I'll tell you, it's happened ten thousand times over the course of my career—a customer will come up to me and kid me, "You know, Jack, you serve the world's most expensive cup of free coffee." Some quietly say, "Wow, before I got out of here, that cup of coffee cost me two thousand dollars."

Before there was a Mitchells clothing store, there was a Mitchell family. So we know what it's like to take kids along when you shop. To keep them occupied and out of your hair, we have a television set by the soft drinks with a VCR attached. If there's nothing they like on

TV, we show them one of their favorite movies. We also have a basketful of lollipops at Mitchells to keep them happy while they watch the movie. Make the kids happy and you make the parents happy. Nobody at Mitchells or Richards ever says, "Will you please get your kid to stop that." They're our guests too. Bill likes to watch the sporting events, but there were always kids glued to Bugs Bunny or the Roadrunner, so he put a second TV up on the wall to catch the football or basketball game.

Dad loves to tell the story of the time Paul Newman came in many years ago with his four-year-old daughter. Mom plopped her on her lap and read stories to her while Paul shopped. When he was done, he came to collect her, but she wouldn't budge. "No, I like it here too much," she said. Finally, he had to bribe her to leave by offering to buy her a new bicycle, which did the trick. For years afterward, Paul kidded Mom and Dad that shopping at the store had cost him a bicycle.

Whenever I notice customers shopping with young children, I like to go over and kneel down so I'm at child height and say, "Hi there, I just wanted to thank you for bringing your mom and dad into the store today."

Getting back to my house analogy, I think of the shoe department as the living room, because that's the one place where you can sit down. And I suppose the fitting rooms are the bedrooms. From the first time someone steps into the store, I try to convey this homey feel. Wouldn't you like to feel the same way when you stop in at the insurance agent or the lamp store?

Chapter 7

Know the Dog's Name Too

If you're going to hug each customer like a friend, you have to really get to know them. And I don't mean just the obvious things, but the details. You can't have someone show up who's bought from you five or six times, and not remember the customer's name. Imagine instead how *you'd* feel if you walked into a store and the sales associate who last waited on you strolled up with a big smile and said, "Hey Rob, great to see you again." Better yet, imagine how you'd feel if he followed that up by asking, "So, how's Rickee, and how are little Mark and Jennifer?" Even better, imagine if he then said, "How're you doing with that navy Zegna suit you bought here last March? We just got a beautiful one in the other day, a gray pinstripe, and we have one in your size, 44 Long."

Now that's *knowing* your customer. How many businesses could pull that off on a daily basis?

We do, because we maintain a database with detailed profiles of over 115,000 customers. We know every item a customer has ever purchased and when they purchased it, going back years. We know their sizes, their brand preferences, their style preferences, and their color preferences. We often know their nicknames, family names, birthdays, anniversaries, hobbies, where they work, where their spouses work, their golf handicaps, whatever bits of information they're willing to share that would be useful to maintain a personal connection. If a customer comes in and mentions she's in a bit of a rush because she has to fetch her dog at the vet, we'll say, "Oh, sorry to hear that, is Lucia okay?" We know the dog's name too.

We gather all this information not by taking formal surveys or subjecting them to an interrogation (although we do survey customer satisfaction), but by listening and learning during the selling process and developing a personal and professional relationship with them. The principle here is, "Probe, Don't Pry." And customers know us well enough to realize we'd never divulge any personal information.

When a customer calls and says she's coming in to shop and doesn't have a lot of time, she doesn't need a lot of time. Her sales associate will check her profile and pull out an appropriate selection of clothes based on what her past preferences have been. When she arrives, all she has to do is look them over and say yes or no.

You could do this with any product. Wouldn't you like to go into a restaurant and find that they know your tastes? Say you're a teetotaler. You walk in and you don't have to explain for the umpteenth time that you don't drink alcohol when they ask if you'd like to see the wine list. Anyone who doesn't drink hates that. So they offer you a Pepsi, a Sprite, or an iced tea without even asking. Or they know you like onion rings. I'm a sucker for onion rings. I could eat them three meals a day. I'd love it if I walked into a restaurant I had only been to once or twice and the waiter said, "Would you like some onion rings, like you had last time?" I'd be blown away.

And I'd be blown away even more if the waiter said, "Now I know you sat at table seven last time you were here with Linda, but I think you'd really enjoy sitting here by the window at table three."

Know your customer and they'll know to keep coming back.

ſ

Chapter 8

Piling On the Hugs

You can go a long way toward making a very satisfied customer with one simple hug, but the great huggers pile the hugs one on top of another until they've created an entire force field of hugs. The great huggers blitz a customer with hugs—with tender loving care.

One morning an executive phoned Debra Gampel, his regular sales associate, and said he was in a real bind. His boss had just called him and said he had to be in Switzerland the next day to lead a seminar on customer service. He went to his closet and, much to his dismay, saw he needed major help. If he was going to look the part, he needed two suits, a sport jacket and all the accessories. And he needed them by five o'clock that day. It was then ten o'clock. Debra told him Don't worry, come on over and I'll have just what you need. That was Hug No 1. She went to the computer and called up his profile to find out his sizes and style preferences. When he arrived to be fitted, Debra had all the clothes picked out—suits, shirts, ties, shoes. All he had to do was nod his approval. He bought almost everything she suggested. She gave him a cup of coffee, and the tailor fitted him. That was Hug No. 2. With twenty-six tailors, it wasn't a problem to have the clothes altered in a few hours. Hug No. 3. He was thrilled, and she gave him a big smile and handshake, and wished him the best on his trip. Hug No. 4. Later that day, the suits were delivered to his home, free of charge. Hug No. 5.

But Debra wasn't done. She raised the bar. She knew from the relationship she had developed with him that it was his birthday the next day. During his last visit, Deb had put his birthday into his profile in the computer and spotted it when she looked up his previous purchases. When he sat down to lead the seminar on customer service in Switzerland, it occurred to him to tell the same-day-delivery story about Mitchells and Debra Gampel. He was wearing one of his new suits and opened the jacket to show the Mitchells label, when he felt an envelope in the breast pocket. He pulled it out and—you know what it was—a birthday card with a personal note from Debra. Big, big Hug No. 6.

When he returned, his first stop was at Mitchells so he could tell me the entire story. When he pulled out that card, he had been so touched that he told the Swiss all about this great associate and the extraordinary service she provides. "And at the end," he said, "the stuffy Swiss bankers actually clapped!"

For Debra, all those hugs were natural. She has the hugging mindset.

Chapter 9

Selling Underwear on Sunday

A lot of businesses really get hung up conforming to what's considered "standard practice" for their industry. If you're in the fast-food business, you don't employ waiters or waitresses. If you're a nightclub, you don't open for lunch. But why should you care about "standard practice" if you're trying to please customers? We're great believers in offering customers a service that might be commonplace in another industry but is a luxury in your business.

People, for instance, have medical emergencies. They have dental emergencies. They also have clothing emergencies. What do you do if you have a clothing emergency and it's midnight? Or it's Sunday? We believe we ought to be the same as doctors and have someone on call at any hour on any day. It was Bill who came up with this idea. We set up a system so if a customer calls Mitchells when it's closed and gets the recorded message, there's an option that if it's an emergency, press 2, and you'll be routed to Bill's home phone in Westport. If he's not in, you press 3 and you get Todd Mitchell. If he's not there, you can get Andrew Mitchell. We have a similar hierarchy at Richards. Then, if someone needs something immediately, Bill will come down to the store and open it up.

The most common after-hours call is when someone forgot to pick up their alterations and it's Sunday morning and they're leaving on a business trip that afternoon. Now there are times when what a customer considers an emergency is hardly what we would regard as an emergency, but that doesn't matter. We do whatever it takes. So no matter what the reason, we'll come down and open up the store. And we do it not only for our good customers, but we also do it for complete strangers.

A few years ago, one of these calls came to Bill's house on a Sunday afternoon. Now at that very moment Bill was really into watching the football game—the playoffs. When Bill picked up the phone, a man whose name he didn't recognize and who had in fact never shopped in our stores said he was in a real bind. He had flown in from Texas for a bar mitzvah and he had somehow forgotten to pack his bow tie and cummerbund for his tuxedo. Everything was closed. Could he help? Bill said he would be glad to. He got up from the couch, clicked off the game, and drove over to meet the man at the store. He found him a bow tie and cummerbund, and the man was effusive in his thanks. Bill had saved his day. My pleasure, Bill told him, and went home to resume watching the game, two touchdowns later. It was only years afterward that we learned the man was a former big shot of Neiman Marcus.

Which brings me to the underwear. One Sunday I needed to go down to Richards to meet some businessmen I was negotiating with on a deal. They came, we went off and toured Greenwich Avenue to talk over our business, and then I returned to the store to pick up my briefcase. It was Sunday and we were closed, but when I got there a couple of men were outside and wondered if they could come in and pick up a few things. One thing I really hate—I think everyone does— is when you show up at a store just after it's closed—you could be one minute too late—and all the "help" is still inside, and some last-minute shoppers, and you rap on the door, but they won't let you in. They ignore you. Why would you go back to that store if there was another convenient alternative? We never do that, and so even though it was just me, I said, fine, come on in. I sold them two suits, a sport coat, and a pair of trousers.

Just as I was leaving, the phone rang. I thought it might be one of my sons seeing how the meeting went, so I picked it up. It was an elderly woman, who said, "I'm desperate. Do you know where I could buy some underwear?" She sounded really frantic. I told her she could find some over at the mall. She said she really didn't like the mall, was there any other place? So I couldn't help but ask her why she was in such a rush to find underwear on Sunday. She said they had sold their Greenwich estate and were moving to a smaller place. The moving van had just been there, and she had packed all of her husband's underwear and he was really annoyed at her. Of course I told her, "Come on over."

Twenty minutes later, she tottered in and bought a few packages of underwear. Hey, every pair of briefs counts. More important, maybe I even saved a marriage.

Chapter 10

Tuxedos to Go

Hugging, if you're really going to exceed your customers' expectations, involves a good deal of flexibility. You have to be willing to go out on a limb and try things you've never tried before. Maybe they won't work, but maybe they'll turn into a spectacular hug. An essential principle of hugging is to be willing to think outside the box.

Take Tuxedos to Go. This was one of the wilder adventures I got involved in, but it proved to be a big winner, both for Mitchells and our client. Years ago, Vince Wasik, now a valued member of our advisory board, was the chief executive of Holland America Lines. He wanted to bring back the mystique and glamour of the days of transatlantic cruises, but he knew it wasn't going to be easy. Whenever he went aboard one of Holland America's Bermuda cruises, he had to wince. When couples came to dinner, the women would be dressed in gowns and look great, but the men would invariably be in their casual best. Some of them looked like they were going to the junior prom. Anytime the Dutch owners took in this scene, they would go ballistic. They couldn't stand the deterioration in the dress code.

Vince wanted to figure out a way to prod the men to dress up. Not only would they look better, but he knew the psychology of clothing. If someone looks good, they feel great. If they feel great, they spend more. He reasoned that if he got the men to dress up as much as the women, then the bar business would improve and the sales in the shops would increase. But how to do it?

Vince bought his own clothes at Mitchells, so he came to Bill and me for help. He actually hired us as consultants, and I went with Mel Gross, my senior buyer, on one of the Bermuda cruises. Actually, we were so busy that we flew down to Bermuda and met the ship there and took it back. We found something in the bowels of the ship that Vince didn't even know about—a tailor shop. It mended the draperies and took care of the crew's uniforms. And we hatched the idea of Tuxedos to Go. The way it would work was, when a couple arrived on the ship, the cabin steward would escort them to their cabin and show them how everything worked. Before taking his leave, he would hand the man an invitation from the captain that offered him a tuxedo to wear during the cruise. We would have a full range of tuxedos and shirts on board, and the tailors would alter them to fit. We had Domenic train the tailors so they could do it rapidly with the proper equipment.

Now, the Dutch owners thought Vince was crazy to try this. The clientele was already stealing the cheese boards and ashtrays faster than the crew could replace them. Lend them tuxedos? They'd steal every one of them! But Vince prevailed, and we gave it a shot. We called up Lord West and ordered five hundred tuxedos, the biggest tuxedo order we had ever made, and put the program into place on one of the cruises.

When the men opened up the invitations, they didn't know quite what to make of them; in many cases, they had never worn a tuxedo before, particularly one that actually fit. But the wives were thrilled at the prospect of seeing their husbands all dolled up. They made them go and get fitted. The incredible thing is, the couples boarded the ship at 4 P.M. and we had their tuxedos altered and back to them in time for the captain's dinner the next evening.

One thing we didn't do is provide shoes, because it's kind of hard to tailor shoes. We didn't anticipate what we saw on those first cruises, which was men coming down to dinner in tuxedos with brown shoes or even sneakers. But when they sat down at their tables, the guys looked magnificent. Vince got notes from the wives that were effusive in their praise: "This is the second happiest day of my life. The first was my wedding day." All of a sudden, bar sales exploded. Sales shot up at the shops. The guests looked great, so they felt great and they spent great. It was incredible. Travel agents came on the ships and were so impressed by how everyone looked that they pushed Holland America Lines cruises more than ever. The ships were booked solid all summer.

It turned out that some of the men did steal the tuxedos along with the cheese boards, but that was fine. The next time they booked a cruise, they didn't have to be fitted.

Chapter 11

The Return Hug

When you hug often enough, you find that your customers hug back. They smile at you. They send you notes. They say nice things to friends and turn them into customers. That's significant. That's the evidence that a true relationship has formed. There's a bond. And it means your hug worked.

A woman wrote me just the other day: "I am absolutely impressed! I was in Richards on Friday, shopping with Belinda Cole, and received a thank-you note from you by Monday—wow! And I haven't even sent my thank-you notes for my new baby daughter's gifts!"

An investment banker, not a regular Mitchell's customer, was in the Westport store during our end-of-summer sale. He and his wife each bought some items at half price and were pleased at the bargains they got. A few days later, as I do with most big sales, I sent him a handwritten thank-you note and made mention of the specific things he had bought. He was so amazed by this that he took the note into a company meeting as an example of how customers should be treated. Then he e-mailed me and all his associates his appreciation, and said he felt so guilty being showered with such attention when he was a one-time sale customer that he was looking forward to stopping by to buy some things at full price. I loved the hug back!

Phyllis Bershaw can barely keep up with all the return hugs she gets for the remarkable service she provides. The other day, one of her faithful customers stopped at the druggist to pick up some medication for Phyllis. That's right, customers run errands for Phyllis to save *her* time. A few years ago, a restaurant owner whose wife is a loyal customer wanted to show his appreciation and so he named a salad after her, the "Phyllis." It's delicious.

So, remember, everyone loves a hug, and everyone loves a hug back. Try it today. Do it now, go for it!

HUGGING STUDY GUIDE #1

Huggers sell with passion so they develop long-term personal and loyal relationships with customers—this means seeing, listening, and caring about the customer, and treating the customer as your friend.

You have to develop extremely satisfied customers—in the new business landscape, it's no longer enough to have satisfied customers.

Customer-centric organizations are the best huggers—that's because they're always thinking about hugs; everyone, from top to bottom, focuses first on the customer, the center of the universe. Everyone hugs and everyone sells.

A hug is anything that exceeds a customer's expectations—it's a mindset. There is no one way to hug; it can be a smile, a high five, expedited service, or sending out 3-cent stamps.

Everyone on the floor—this is a Golden Principle, because it puts everyone where they can see, touch, and feel real live customers.

Your business should feel like a home—customers should be addressed by first names, there should be coffee and snacks, and there should be diversions for the kids.

Know everything about your customers—you need to truly understand them and learn all you can about them, including the name of a customer's parrot; you listen, you learn, you hug.

Offer services common in other industries but not in yours—that way customers feel as if they're being treated to a luxury.

Think outside the box—take on adventures. In a hugging culture, you need to think imaginatively, and that helps you stay ahead of the competition.

When you hug often enough, customers will hug back—that tells you that your hugs worked and a true relationship has blossomed and they trust you.

PART TWO

From Three Suits to Three Thousand

Evolving a Hugging Organization

Chapter 12

Caring about People
Comes First

In a sense, everything—the stores, the fresh coffee, the hugging—began with ulcers.

When I was growing up, my parents lived in Westport, which was then a much different town than it is today. Not only was it quite a bit smaller, but it was also less affluent, though even then it was a special place. The community consisted of old Yankee farmers, Italian immigrants who built the railroads, plus a cadre of world-class artists and movie and theater celebrities. It was pretty diverse, and there was a core group of sleepy-eyed businessmen who boarded the train to New York City. For most of his business life, my dad was one of those commuters. When he wasn't reading the paper as he rode back and forth, he dreamed, as many of his commuting pals did, of having his own little business and never having to get on the train again.

Dad had climbed up, down, and around the corporate ladder, sampling a variety of jobs, but mostly he worked in marketing and advertising in the big city. By the time he had entered his early fifties, though, the stress of corporate life was really taking its toll on him. He had suffered from terrible ulcers during his forties. Many a night he would be up in awful pain, and there was one Thanksgiving when he rose from the dinner table and said, "I've got to go to the hospital, because I know I'm bleeding." In fifth grade, I remember having to do a biology project and decided to write about ulcers and the five operations on my father's insides. My classmates found it fascinating, though I know Dad and Mom didn't find ulcers terribly interesting.

One day, when I was just a freshman at Wesleyan University, Dad called me and announced that he was giving up the rat race and starting a store. Dad, in his former life, did some retail consulting, so he knew a bit about the techniques of operating a store. "Wow, Dad," I said. "Think about this for a minute. This is a big move. Come up and let's talk." Mom and Dad drove up the next day to Middletown, and they explained their plan. Mom had the positive phrase that I will always remember: "If we do it, let's do it together."

Ulcers might have been the catalyst that got Dad thinking about starting a store, but the reason he was an ideal person to do it was because he cared about people. And that's key to evolving a hugging organization. You can't be a hugger if you don't like people and sincerely care about them. Especially if you're the boss. Because your personality becomes the business.

There are people that are warm and caring with their family and friends, and then arrogant and crass with their customers. You can't have two philosophies, one for your life and one for your business. Your customers must become an extension of your family.

Dad always had a smile and a good word for everybody even if he was having a bad day. If someone was down in the dumps, he would always try to cheer them up. Which was easy for him, because all of his stories—and he had plenty of them—were always upbeat.

I'm constantly struck by how many people in the service industry obviously don't care about people. A friend of mine told me about this encounter with a local garage. He was standing outside one of the bays while the oil was changed in his car. A few other customers were waiting while other mechanics worked on their cars. A man drove up and politely asked the owner, "My dog ran away, and I think he might have headed this way. He's a brown lab. Did you happen to notice a dog going by?"

The owner gave the man a cold look and snorted, "I'm under cars all day. I'm not looking out at the road."

He made the man feel like a fool, when all he had to do was say, "Gee, I'm sorry, I haven't seen any. I hope you find him." It wouldn't have taken any longer. Do you think that man will ever become a customer? My friend was so outraged by the unnecessary rudeness that he decided right then and there he was never coming back, even though the garage was the most convenient one to his home. And think of the example that man set for his employees.

That garage owner didn't care about the dog or its owner. Perhaps he thought that customers come to him simply because he cares about cars. Of course they do come to him because he cares about cars, but they usually come back if he also demonstrates that he cares about them.

You can teach people how to replace an oil filter or how to alter a suit, but you can't teach them how to care. That comes from within. I'm not saying everyone has to care about people. But if you don't, try becoming a lobster fisherman or choose a business other than the service industry.

Chapter 13

It's Not Location, Location, Location— It's Service, Service, Service

When Dad quit his job, his idea was to open the store in Florida, since it was less hectic and perfect for a quality-of-life change. With Mom's blessings, Dad decided to sell the house in Westport. It was 1958. Dad was fifty-three. My brother Bill was in his first year at Staples High School. I was in my first year at Wesleyan. We both wondered if it would really work or whether Dad had lost it.

Our house was put on the market, and my mother stayed to sell it while my father scouted around Florida for the best location for the store. One day, Mom was showing the house to an executive from Mobil Oil. Sweeney—I will never forget that name. As he and his wife wandered through the rooms, his wife asked Mom where she could find clothes for her husband and four sons in Westport, and the light-bulb went on—there were only one or two little stores in town. As soon as the couple left, she called my father and told him, "Let's start the store in Westport. There's a need, and we have lived here forever. We know everybody in town, and if we're good, they'll buy from us here."

I always wondered what would have happened if Mrs. Sweeney hadn't raised the subject of clothes shopping, but life's turns often result from chance events. Dad returned from Florida, they took the house off the market, and they began sizing up the available commercial properties in Westport. They settled on an eight-hundred-square-foot space that had been the storefront display area of Dickson Heating and Plumbing and Supply, located in a small, nondescript building at the corner of Post Road and North Compo. Dickson kept the back to store its pipes and faucets, and Dad had the front.

Now that wasn't the best spot in town, by any stretch of the imagination. It was what Dad and Mom could afford. But they were shrewd enough to understand another important concept for evolving a hugging organization. If you are able to deliver exceptional customer service, you don't need to have the best location.

Like everyone else, I've heard this "location, location, location" spiel, ad nauseam. Well, our take has always been unconventional. You don't want to choose the worst possible location, buried ten miles into the woods next to the town dump. But a decent location—meaning reasonable traffic, convenient to get to, and more than adequate parking—will do just fine if you learn to hug.

The same principle applies to inventory. When the store opened, there were a few dozen shirts, some socks, a couple of sweaters, and a few ties. Plus exactly three Doncaster suits, the brand Dad created for the store, priced at $65 apiece. A size 40 banker's stripe. A 42 navy blue. And a 42 charcoal gray. When I share the three-suits story, people today are simply amazed. Nowadays we stock over three thousand suits—for men and women. There's no more Doncaster, but we have all the top brands, from Zegna to Armani to Hickey-Freeman to Canali, and a dash more than $65.

That original inventory wasn't much, but it didn't have to be. Not if your focus is on customer service. Dad and Mom decided to round up customers, care for them, and then build the inventory.

Even at that early stage, they understood that customers wanted five things more than they wanted a great location or enormous inventory:

1. A friendly greeting
2. Personal interest
3. A business that makes them feel special
4. A "no problem" attitude
5. Forward thinking

Since my parents had lived in Westport for many years, the first customers were old friends—people from the neighborhood, friends we saw in church, others from Boy Scouts and the YMCA and Dad's involvement in Westport. The first database was actually our family Christmas-card list. Mom and Dad sent out a little note to everyone on the list sharing that he wasn't riding the train anymore, he was running a men's and boys' clothing store. In his original flyer, Dad actually wrote a poem about how he had given up riding the train. Maybe it was a little corny, very folksy, but it meant that we were beginning a very personal, very down-to-earth, only-in-America business. Once they exhausted the Christmas-card list, they moved on to the Westport phone book, one-on-one marketing in its infancy. That kept us busy for a while.

It was natural for Mom and Dad to treat our first customers as friends, because they literally were our friends. But my parents were the same way with perfect strangers who wandered in. That's why a coffeepot was always on—and still is. I guess you could say the place was about as homey as you could get. One day a customer walked in and noticed my mother sitting there darning a sock. "Do you have a vendor problem or something?" he asked. "No," she replied. "One of the things we do for customers is stitch name tags on their socks for camp or prep school."

My parents called the store Ed Mitchell. Simple as that, my father's name. (It was a different era; today I am sure it would be Norma and Ed Mitchell's.) And the store was simple, and very much a family enterprise. Everyone pitched in with typical entrepreneurial spirit. During the day, Mom took care of the coffee. She had never worked after graduating from Smith, but since she had majored in economics, she kept "the books" at night. Dad was the store salesman, buyer, and janitor. Bill helped after school and on weekends.

My grandmother, my father's mother, who we called Nani, was skilled enough to serve as the store's tireless tailor and seamstress. When Dad needed a pair of trousers cuffed, he would scoot over to her place and in thirty minutes she'd have them ready. Today, there are twenty-six tailors in Westport and another sixteen in our Greenwich store. Wouldn't Nani be proud!

And when my parents came to visit me, they would pack the brown station wagon full of sweaters, blazers, shoes, even underwear, and schlep around to the Wesleyan fraternity houses and sell to the frat members. This was one more form of intimate service—bringing the store to the customers. We might sell a few hundred dollars' worth of merchandise, and that was a good day. Listen, every Shetland sweater counted.

"I think the single thing that helped us was our service," Dad liked to say. "Almost anything you wanted, we did it. We never said no."

And from the minute Mom and Dad opened the store, Dad never had one more ulcer.

Chapter 14

The Three Principles
of Expansion

Our store did about $50,000 worth of business the first year. It didn't worry Macy's or Brooks Brothers, but my parents were thrilled by a very promising start.

As business steadily improved, it became obvious we needed more space. So my parents convinced Dickson Plumbing to move its wall back and that got them another hundred square feet. Then when the Westport National Bank building went up, we moved down there. We kept taking more and more space, until finally, in 1979, we moved into the beautiful freestanding building we now occupy, which has grown to more than 33,000 square feet. We still don't have the best location, but as I said, we don't need it.

Dad and Mom, however, did recognize that there were three key principles of expansion if you were going to evolve a hugging organization:

1. **Give new management people responsibility and authority.**
When you expand, you have to bring in additional management so you're not spread too thin. It was logical for Dad and
Mom to turn first to their sons, but they understood that
whether you're a family business or any business, you have to
give your new management a sense of responsibility and authority or they will never fully embrace the hugging culture.

Their first recruit, in 1965, was Bill. To ensure that Bill felt
totally involved, Mom and Dad made it clear that he was in
every sense their full partner. They sold alongside each other,
which made Bill feel great, and at day's end, they vacuumed
the floor alongside each other, which made Bill feel a little
less great. But he appreciated the fact that he was not an adjunct of the business, but part of its essence.

It's literally impossible to imagine Mitchells without Bill
flying around the selling floor. He connects with customers in
such an endearing and genuine way, and makes everyone he
talks to feel like the most important person in the world. Long
before extraordinary customer service became a buzz phrase,
or I started to use the word "hugging," Bill was living and
breathing it. He's the turn-to guy, Mr. Westport, the man who
makes the floor sing. He is always ready, willing, and able to
pick up the phone late at night or on Sundays to help out
when Mitchells is closed. Sue, his wife, says, "He has his car
turned to head out like an EMT ready to react to any and all
emergencies."

I'm a very straight arrow, predictable, and tend, I am told,
to overthink things. Bill is conceptual and highly intuitive. He
effortlessly makes people feel terrific. He's truly the heart and

soul of our business. And he's the most generous person I've ever known. Born a world-class hugger.

The funny thing is, I never intended to join the business. I used to think, if you sell one suit or dress, you've sold them all, and even today my passion is the people, not the clothes. After receiving a bachelor of arts from Wesleyan, I earned a master's degree at the University of California at Berkeley in Chinese history and culture in 1963, and thought about becoming a diplomat. I had this hidden desire to become the first ambassador to China. By the time I finished my studies, however, the United States was still not speaking to China. Plus, I believe, I am slightly dyslexic and was an absolutely terrible language student. The demand for Chinese diplomats remained nil, and so I had to find something else to do. After a brief six months working for Dad, I got a job as an administrator at a research institute in Ridgefield, Connecticut, a small nonprofit company engaged in basic research.

By 1969, with four sons to feed, and with the institute having a tough time of it because funding was drying up for basic research, Linda and I were struggling. Dad and Bill had some bold new aspirations for the store. They were selling men's and boys' clothing, but boys, many of whom were heading to communes, were wearing jeans and sandals, and if they wore the same jeans five days in a row, all the better. Women were coming in with their husbands, or in many cases coming in alone to buy clothes for their husbands, but they couldn't buy anything for themselves. It made a lot of sense to start a women's department.

So, in 1969, Bill made a specific proposal for me to join

and run the women's side of it. This appealed to me, because it meant a challenge to begin something new, something of which I would have "ownership." I said yes, though, to be honest, I really didn't think I would like it. To my surprise, I absolutely, positively, passionately loved it from the second I walked in.

2. **Don't build a mountain.** As more people joined the business, Dad had to think hard about organization. There was never any doubt in his mind that he wasn't going to go down the road of bureaucracy and hierarchy.

   We're convinced that to hug effectively you need to have a flat organization that doesn't have much in the way of hierarchy. You simply can't have a hugging culture in a bureaucracy. Bureaucracy kills warmth and openness. It doesn't allow for a culture of always being open to new ideas. In our business, we don't stress an organizational chart or chain of command or channels. Our structure is almost a little bit disorganized. You don't want something that looks like a mountain that associates feel they have to climb. A flat organization, we feel, is a hug to everyone who works there.

   We've always striven for an environment that is open and honest. We don't check up on people or put them down for not selling the extra suit or dress. Rather, we concentrate on giving them new ideas of how they might have done it differently. It was that way in the early days, and it's still that way. Judy Brooks, a wonderful new associate, shared with me the other day: "I just love it here. You guys let me grow at my own pace, in my own way, hugging me to be me. And I get up each morning loving to come to work." And you know, Judy's business has been on fire. She is passing on the hugs we've given her to her customers.

3. **Remember where you came from.** No matter how big you get, you can't forget your roots and what got you where you are. Otherwise, you become a different organization. Many businesses start out with certain come-ons—free this or free that—and then once they feel they've got plenty of customers, those free services suddenly are no longer free. We have never operated that way. For instance, everyone has always gotten free alterations. We believe what's good for the goose is good for the gander. If men get free alterations, women should too. I can't imagine how other high-end stores can look Mrs. Smith in the eye and tell her that her alterations cost $50 to $200 when Mr. Smith's alterations are free. Our feeling is that when you buy clothes that say Mitchells or Richards on the label, the least we can do is make sure they fit impeccably. As we like to say, every *body* is different, and you should not pay extra for the difference!

And you know those signs you see all the time, even in the best of stores: "Your alterations will be ready March 25," which is usually two weeks after the day you're standing on the fitting stool? You won't see them in our stores, no matter how busy we get. Our mindset is, "When does the customer need the dress or sport coat—tonight or tomorrow, or is two weeks okay?"

We had an orthopedic surgeon stop in once and he got beeped and asked if he could use our phone (this was before even five-year-olds had cellphones), and we said of course. After he made his call, five yards from where he was standing, he mentioned that he had been in a fancy store in New York and he got beeped and the salesperson said, "Sure, the phone's one floor down and around the corner." He went down and it was a pay phone, and he had no change, so he had to go back upstairs and change a bill. Can you imagine? Ticking off a customer for a lousy quarter! The good doctor never returned. Fortunately, he found us—who haven't forgotten where we came from.

Chapter 15

Get No. 1 and You'll Get No. 1,000

We were doing fine in the early 1970s, but then something beyond our own expectations happened that pushed us to new heights. GE moved its corporate headquarters from New York City to Fairfield County, becoming the first big company to locate in our neck of the woods. As it happened, Reginald Jones, then the chief executive, and his wife, Grace, already shopped at our store and were good friends. Reg came in one day and said to Dad, Bill, and me, "You'd better put a new wing on the store, because we're all going to shop here." And, boy, was he was right. Hardly a day went by without GE guys passing through the store hunting for suits. GE liked to bring good things to life; well, it brought a lot of good customers to us.

The surge of customers taught us the power of No. 1. People looking to rise in an organization pay close attention to everything about their immediate boss, and particularly the chief executive. If he happens to wear Hickey-Freeman suits, they figure it couldn't hurt to wear the same thing. If he shops at Mitchells, it couldn't hurt if they shopped there too. So we began actively courting chief executives, presidents, and owners of companies.

Often these business leaders would tell us about how they didn't have the time or clothes knowledge to find the right outfits. Don't worry, we told them, we'll make it easy. They could make appointments to get fitted. They could come in after hours, or before hours. And we'd be happy to come to their office, even if their office was in New York or New Jersey, and fit them right there. They loved it.

Every time a new chief executive became a customer, flocks of other managers from the same company soon showed up at our door wanting to look like the big guy. The GE connection continued as Reg passed the torch to Jack Welch and more recently to Jeff Immelt.

We always stitched an "Ed Mitchell" label inside our suits in addition to the manufacturer's brand. When an up-and-coming GE manager saw the label of the chief executive's suit, and it said "Ed Mitchell," it told him where to go to get his clothes.

In time, more and more corporations gravitated to nearby cities— IBM came to Armonk, New York, Xerox came to Stamford, and others followed—and by courting the top officers many of their employees, and spouses, became our customers. (At the same time, we continued to serve the local firefighters and clergy and artists.)

Once we had these connections at the top, we were able to seize on all sorts of little opportunities for extra business. We always kept our eyes open, and looked beyond the obvious. For instance, GE ran lots of tours of its headquarters for groups of shareholders, and the tour guides needed outfits. GE would tell the guides what they were supposed to wear and give them a clothing allowance.

We went to top management and told them it would be so easy if we furnished all of the clothing. The guides wouldn't have to go shopping on their own, and we would give GE a corporate discount. For us, it meant repeat business we could count on. So we sold them the outfits—blue double-knit blazers for the male guides and blue double-knit pant suits for the women (remember those double-knit days).

GE also had a corporate fleet of jets that flew out of the Westchester Airport. We sold GE the uniforms for its pilots—blue blazers and gray pants. We learned that Mobil Oil had an even bigger fleet and twenty-five pilots. Mobil wanted its pilots to look like executives so it gave each of them four suits a year. We sold them the suits, a hundred a year.

When you get No. 1, you get No. 1,000.

Chapter 16

Hug Your Way Over the Bumps

No matter how hard you hug your customers, you're still going to hit some bumps. Treacherous circumstances beyond your control—like recessions—come around every so often and can wreck a business. Nobody enjoys sinking sales, and cutbacks inevitably have to be made, but if you're a true hugging organization, it's vital that you make your cuts where the customers don't feel them.

In the early nineties, we experienced our own "worst of times"— the worst economy we had ever faced. Our inventory was out of control. So were expenses. Sales were decreasing rapidly. The quality of our accounts receivable was deteriorating and some of our key clients were going through bankruptcy.

We needed help.

Our advisory board made a powerful recommendation that we hire a strong financial executive to assist Bill and me. The fact that we were visionaries and hard workers was not enough. My eldest son, Russell, joined the business, followed soon after by my son Bob and my wife Linda. Within a year and a half, Russ had addressed the financial issues, and Bob and Linda had focused on our inventory and sales. They worked very closely with Bill and me, and we developed a fabulous professional synergistic working relationship that we spoke of as "the best of times."

We made important adjustments but were careful not to do anything that would affect the customer. For instance, I began signing every check that we wrote for a period of six months. It's amazing how much unnecessary spending you can avoid when the boss signs the checks. Like overtime. Even if you say, "No overtime," it still happens. Associates get sloppy and aren't as productive as they could be. Once I started signing the checks, overtime stopped. Bill and I cut our own salaries significantly. We eliminated all travel. We discontinued things like "brand advertising," which was designed more to build pride in our brand than to touch customers. We began looking at all categories of inventory on a monthly basis with an outside consultant.

We probably would have gone out of the women's business if not for Linda, who had been a seasoned buyer in her family business. Many talented associates contributed to our remarkable growth in the women's business. But without Linda it would never have happened. The margins were low, but Linda turned it around. She was the one that dug in, bought the collections, and did the numbers.

Together, our plan enabled us not only to survive, but also to be in a position to thrive. Within two years we were preparing to expand the Westport store, and by the fall of 1993 we had expanded the selling floor by over 40 percent.

As part of the face-lift, we changed the name of the store from Ed

Mitchell to Mitchells. A lot of our business was now women's clothing. We did some focus-group interviews, and the women said "Ed Mitchell" sounded too masculine. The other thing was, Mitchells represented the whole family, not just one man, and that felt right to us. That's why there's no apostrophe before the "s."

By hugging our way over the bumps, we actually emerged from the adversity so strong that we began to think about having a second store. In 1995, we took the plunge and bought the leading men's store in Greenwich, called Richards. It was a powerhouse, doing over $10 million in a cramped, eight-thousand-square-foot, cluttered environment that, from a visual perspective, violated every principle of upper-end retailing. Yet there was a great spirit among the sales associates and their customers. The sales associates were huggers, yet they were back one generation with Mom and Dad when it came to systems and follow-up. They had enormous potential, they just hadn't realized it yet.

When you make an acquisition, you can be sure you're going to hit some new bumps, and we did. The big one was that the Richards associates were terrified that their jobs were in jeopardy. And we didn't know if the Richards customers would desert us. In Westport, there was trepidation among our Mitchells associates and customers that we might pay less attention to them. In short, there was a lot of anxiety in the air.

So we navigated these bumps by applying our hugging philosophy to the deal in every way. We kept the name Richards, a great brand name in Greenwich, as a symbol of our commitment to the Richards customers to maintain the hometown spirit of their store. In our public relations and marketing letter to our new Greenwich customers, we used the word "merging" rather than "acquiring," and spoke of the "Perfect Pair."

Quietly behind the scenes, my son Todd Mitchell introduced our hugging computer systems; plus, more important, Russ and Bob spent 80 percent of their time in Greenwich hugging our new associates and reassuring them that the future would be fun and profitable for them. Over the next five years, we almost doubled the business in the very same space, and industry leaders told us we probably were doing more per square foot than any men's store in the country. We are most proud that we didn't lose a single veteran Richards hugger, save one who left for an entirely different career. Plus our customers in Westport told us, "Wow, you did all this in Greenwich and didn't lose a beat with us in Westport."

From the beginning, we knew we would have to move to a new building to really grow, and soon after buying Richards, we signed an option on a piece of property across the street. Four years later, on September 9, 2000, we opened the new Richards building, and under Bill's son Scott we introduced women's wear for the first time. The hallmark of the store is a flying limestone staircase in the center that leads to the women's clothing on the second floor. I call it the stairway to heaven. Richards won the award for Store of the Year for the world for 2000 in the annual Retail Design Awards competition.

The thing we are most proud of is the "loyalty award" we won that came from our longtime customers who said they felt really comfortable in this new, updated home.

And one of the most remarkable things is that Ed Schachter, the former owner of Richards, continues to work in the store, with the same intensity and enthusiasm, and hugs customers as if he were still the owner. We continue to call him "the boss." It's our way of hugging him for selling us his business. He doesn't need to hug customers anymore, he just loves to. And that's not what happens when most owners sell their businesses.

Chapter 17

The Family Rules

Many family businesses and marriages have been tested and sometimes broken due to lack of communication on issues generated by the business. One thing we worried about was a frightening fact: 92 percent of all family businesses don't get past the third generation. That means only 8 percent do. A scary statistic!

Bill and I have seven children between us, all sons, and like all fathers, naturally we dreamed they might one day come into our business, but we were not sure how to successfully do that. We both felt strongly it would have to be their decision, not ours.

So Bill, Linda, and I really focused on preserving family harmony and setting things up so the business would continue not just for three generations but, if we're lucky, dozens of generations. Having the next generation follow successfully and synergistically is, to my mind, the greatest hug of all and will be the greatest legacy of my business life.

In the mid-eighties, at a menswear conference in Minneapolis, Bill and I met David Bork, an astute family-business consultant. After David's presentation, Bill said to me, "Jack, hire him. I like him. He's bright. Hire him!" And we did—quickly.

David began helping Bill and me iron out our roles before we tackled the next generation. It took a year or two, and many "tough love" meetings, but in the end we became a much stronger and bonded brother partnership.

We formed an outside advisory board consisting of five outside advisors plus the Mitchells that were active in the business. Its members include senior executives from various disciplines and professions, and all friends and fans of our family and business. We pay them, we meet quarterly, and this advisory board has forced us to be more disciplined and businesslike.

Their first contribution was to help us formalize two "rules" that governed the entry of our seven sons into the business. You know by now I hate rules. But these principles were really in cement, so Bill and I labeled them rules.

The rules apply just as well to owners of businesses that aren't family businesses who bring friends or friends of friends into their business. Too often, entrepreneurs add people to their business as favors without weighing the possible consequences.

So here are our rules:

1. **Five years elsewhere.** The first rule is that each son has to work somewhere else for at least five years after graduation from college. Bill, Linda, and I had seen so many family businesses fail because the father or the mother wanted their off-

spring to come in immediately, no experience, just entitled by birth. I remember there was a club in the menswear business—S.O.B.'s, or "Sons of Bosses"—and 98.6 percent of the sons were always complaining about their fathers not listening to their "good ideas." I remember thinking that some of the ideas were great, and the fathers felt they knew it all because their sons were just kids—what did they know?

2. **A real job.** The second rule is that when they join the business, it has to be for a real job for which they are qualified. They can't just displace someone. As Bork pointed out to us, there's no correlation between competence and the family gene pool. So you have to manage the boundaries between the business and the family. In a family, you should be accepted unconditionally. But in a business, your acceptance is conditioned on your suitability for the job. The driving force is performance, the bottom line, and you can't forget that.

Another principle we live by is that when a decision has to be made, the primary consideration is what is right for the business, not what is just right for the family. If you do it the other way around, you're dooming your business. It's a fundamental family business paradigm: What is right for the business is right for the family.

All four of our sons—Russell, Bob, Todd, and Andrew—and Bill's son Scott, who refer to themselves as G3, their shorthand for third generation, have followed our rules of putting in time elsewhere for at least five years and joining us when there was a real job available.

We're hoping Bill's remaining two, if they want to, will join us too, when there's a "real job" for them.

For twelve years now, we have had the discipline of meeting almost every Tuesday with every one of the active Mitchells for an hour or two, or sometimes more. I chair the meeting, with a written agenda. I'm a consensus leader, so I let a lot of people talk and get their feelings out, and there are a lot of opinions, but there is a magic to this discipline of two hours a week, all together discussing the major challenges to the business.

About three years ago, we re-engaged David Bork with the idea that he could facilitate the process of succession: Who of the G3s would be the executive function as we passed the business on to the next generation? It took us three years to unanimously agree that Russ and Bob would share the roles as co-presidents and eventually become co-CEOs. For the moment, I remain CEO and chairman, while Bill is vice chairman. There are many reasons why we are all so confident that these two young men will work together in a synergistic manner to build our business to new heights. All of us recognize that, bone deep, they are super huggers. They understand customer first.

Over that three-year period, we had many, many meetings and discussions, and we even set up an additional, very important new institution, which we call the Family Council. Composed of all Mitchells, their spouses, and their children over the age of fourteen, the council meets quarterly, chaired by a Mitchell not active in the business, and tries to separate the business issues from the family issues.

All told, there are now nine Mitchells in the business, including Dad, who at ninety-eight still comes into the store on Saturday. Every time I say to someone, "Can you imagine having all of your family in the business?"—pause—"We're talking about my four sons, my brother, his oldest son, my dad, and, most important, Linda, my wife," I have to pinch myself. All in the business, all getting along, all having fun, all hugging customers. When I talk to people, especially anyone in a family business, they find it mind-boggling. They just say, "Wow! I can't imagine it!"

Chapter 18

Today Half the Closet,
Tomorrow Every Hanger

I like to say that our customers "think global, but shop local."

Over 80 percent of our customers live within a fifteen-mile radius. This is because people like to shop locally. As Tip O'Neill said, all politics is local. All shopping is local if you have world-class products and world-class service.

Even though almost all of our customers live in Fairfield and Westchester Counties, they travel the globe, same as the customers of any business. Many of them work in New York City or visit the city often. They can shop on Madison Avenue and Fifth Avenue. They can shop on Savile Row or Via Montenapoleone.

One of the most important ways we grow is by convincing them that everything they can get in the stores on those streets they can get at Mitchells or Richards—and more. We've heard our customers say that they could buy the same suit or same dress at Saks or Neiman

Marcus, but they prefer working with our sales associates. As a client said to me recently, "Even your tailors know me and hug me. Domenic, Tullio, Pat, Jean, Josephine, Sylvia, Nasra, and Phoung make my wife and me feel special."

Our vision is to own every hanger in everyone's closet. If we were a car dealer, our vision would be to own every garage. If we were a food store, it would be to own every shelf in the refrigerator. Now we're not naïve. We weren't born yesterday. But that's our goal.

Like all businesses, we want more customers, which means more market share, but the main thing we strive for is more business from our existing customers, which means more market scope. That translates to me as greater percentage of closet. We know our customers buy elsewhere. But we're always reaching, searching for new ways to hug and further build a relationship so we can have 100 percent of their closet. Once a relationship gets really deep, a customer who bought dresses from you and scarves and sweaters from somewhere else will start buying the scarves and sweaters from you too.

Many other businesses spend far too much time, money, and energy trying to attract new customers, and don't even know what percentage of closet or shelf or garage they have of their existing customers. As I'll explain later when I talk about technology, we track what people are buying from us and what they aren't. We can check our records and if someone hasn't bought any shoes from us in five years, we don't assume they've begun going barefoot. We know they're shopping elsewhere. So we'll find out what sorts of shoes they like, and if we don't carry them, we'll start carrying them.

Studies show that it costs six times more to get a new customer than it does to keep an existing customer. That's why our focus has always been on better servicing our existing customers.

If you've got half of somebody's closet, shoot for three-quarters and then four-fifths, and before you know it, you'll have every hanger in the closet.

HUGGING STUDY GUIDE #2

You have to like people—you can't evolve a hugging organization if the owner doesn't genuinely like people, because his personality becomes the business.

It's not location, location, location—if you cultivate a hugging culture, you don't need the best location in town or enormous inventory. You need service, service, service.

The three rules of expansion—as you grow, you have to give management people responsibility and authority. You can't build a bureaucratic mountain, and you must not forget the principles on which the business was founded.

Cultivate Number 1—if the top executive of a company becomes your customer, others will follow. It's the power of No. 1.

You have to hug your way over bumps—bad times hit all businesses, and when they do, you can't cut back things that the customer will notice.

If your business is a family business, you need to separate the business issues from the family issues—our way is business first, family second. Our two guiding principles for family members entering the business are: They need five years of outside work experience, and there has to be a real job opening for them. Consider forming an outside advisory board and a family council.

The most effective way to grow is by broadening your market scope—focus on servicing your existing customers better, so you occupy a greater share of their closet or shelf or garage.

PART THREE

The Big Secret

How to Hire and Retain Great Associates

Chapter 19

People Come First

When Mom and Dad started the business, they didn't have to worry much about employee relations, because there were no employees. It was Mom and Dad and Nani. Very soon they needed to hire someone to help out, and they hired a fellow named Frank Motel, who was a retired salesman from American Brass. He did magic tricks for the kids while Dad did the selling. When Dad was busy or out at the Rotary Club or otherwise engaged in the community, Frank sold a few suits and ties himself.

Frank was our first associate. And Mom and Dad immediately treated him like family, not as "help," because that was our family philosophy from the beginning. They recognized that if they treated him like family, he would treat customers like family.

Eventually, of course, the business kept growing, and we hired a great many salespeople. And as we believed that great service should come before great product, we also realized that great people to give that service must come at the very top of the hierarchy. Our simple little grid became People/Service/Product.

1. People
2. Service
3. Product

That means it's associates first, customers second, and product third.

Why that order? Because you don't give service in a vacuum. People give service. You can have the best service philosophy in the world, but if you don't have great players to execute it, you've lost the game. In fact, whenever you see people giving fabulous service, they really stand out. If you pull into a gas station and the attendant that puts gasoline in your car cleans the windows without being asked, you're impressed. If he does both the front and back windows, you're even more impressed. And if he does the side windows, and does them with a smile, you're totally blown away. You want to climb out of the car and hug the guy. That's someone you'll definitely remember, and you'll want to come back.

We say it all the time: If you put your best players on the field and your players *are* the best, you'll win. Thus we only try to hire and retain *great* people. We want A players, not B and C players, unless they're B and C players who are capable of becoming A players. I think of Frank Gallagi, our top men's sales associate at Richards, who is an A player extraordinaire. A great client/friend of Frank's said, with his finger in my son Bob's face, "You take care of Frank! If he ever left Richards, it would be like going to Disneyland and not seeing Mickey Mouse!"

Chapter 20

Hiring—The Elements of a Great Associate

Over the years, I've had conversations with human resource officers from some of the big corporations, and they've shown me these elaborate manuals that they rely on to guide them in interviewing and hiring people. Often they're hundreds of pages long, with all sorts of complex charts and appendices. I get dizzy reading them. To my way of thinking, it's not necessary to make everything so complicated. I prefer the old K.I.S.S. theory: Keep It Simple, Stupid.

Years ago, Dad told me what he looked for in anyone he hired, and it was a very simple prescription. It made perfect sense then, and it still does, and we've followed it ever since.

There are four key ingredients:

1. **They must be *competent* and *confident.*** It's easy to check competence. People fill out resumes and you can call references and ask questions. To our mind, all successful people are confident, and no one becomes a superstar without confidence. Confident people will always outperform those who are unsure of themselves and their potential. How do you tell if a potential hire has confidence? It's a good sign if he was the top seller at his previous job, or aspired to be the top seller or shipper, or he was one of the top three. We always look down the resume and if we see the person graduated magna cum laude—we don't care if it was Harvard or Norwalk Community College (our great local community college)—that tells us he knows what it takes and loves to excel, to be the best. Same thing if he were captain of the debating team or the football team. He's got that special stuff. If the candidate is in sales and has product knowledge and knows how to wait on a customer, that suggests he's confident. How he talks gives you another signal. We often interview a prospect four or five times, with different managers, just so we get a range of opinions. I always sit in on one or two of them, and associates later tell me there is something special and personal about having the top dog be part of the interview process. It also sets up the hugging relationship.

2. **They must have a *positive attitude.*** A crucial difference between excellence and mediocrity is a positive attitude. And generally you can tell pretty quickly during an interview if someone has a positive attitude. Do they look on life as the glass is half empty or half full? Is it partly cloudy out or partly

sunny? If they see the glass as five-eighths full, or better yet seven-eighths, they really get our attention.

I'm a big believer in the power of positive words. Whenever I ask someone, "Hi, how are you?" the usual response is, "Fine, how are you?" I usually reply, "I feel great!" Which surprises them because they're not used to hearing someone sound so upbeat. And it makes them feel great, or maybe a dash better at least. It's a hug of sorts. I get a lot of kidding about this, but I love to put on the *Mary Poppins* video with the grandkids and hear the lyrics, "In every job that must be done there is an element of fun," and "When you find the fun, snap, the job's a game." The other day I asked my oldest grandson, Lyle, if he knew my favorite song, and he said, "Oh sure, Pops, it's the one that goes, 'You got to get up every morning with a smile on your face.' "

We like it when people talk about an opportunity rather than a problem. I never use the word "problem." It's always opportunities and challenges. Give us resolutions, not problems. And if you have this genuinely positive attitude, you just don't use the word "no." I hate the word "no." It's always "yes, of course," with me. I sometimes give a little speech about the "Of Course" philosophy, and I say, "Of course we will deliver the dress. Of course we will get you a fresh cup of coffee. Of course we will take the package to your car. Of course we will wrap and send your mom's birthday present (even though it was bought at another store)." Of course, of course, of course.

3. **They must have a *passion* to *listen, learn,* and *grow* to be the best!** Passion is so important, because retailing, like any busi-

ness, can be boring at times. You make five calls, ten calls, and you only get two people to even answer. It can be frustrating. So you need people who have a passion to keep learning new things and adapting. We've found that by asking prospective associates to tell stories, you can determine pretty quickly if they have a passion to learn about things. If candidates are passionate about reading and they say they are reading novels one day and nonfiction the next day, that says they're really passionate, because they read a lot. And naturally, it also says they want to learn new things. Ginger Kermian, a great new women's seller at Richards, told me before we hired her how much she loved to paint. Even though I know nothing about art, I could sense her passion. I knew she would bring that passion to our business. She explained that her sense of color helped her put together outfits for customers. That passion impressed me a lot. She was an instant superstar with us.

If they have the passion for reading, tennis, golf, midwiving, their sons and daughters, travel, they can easily learn how to transfer that feeling to embracing customers. It doesn't really matter if an associate came out of a different environment and with a different mindset, so long as he or she has that passion to learn and grow.

Another part of that passion we look for is that the person is interested in a career with us, not just a job. To us, a *job* means that you go from A to Z, and hopefully you do it well, but a *career* means that you do the same sequence, and then you learn to do it better, and you grow. And then you do it better and better and better, and you grow more. The more you become involved, the more committed you become. That's a career. That's what we are looking for—career huggers.

4. **Integrity.** This is the most important principle of all. In fact, I don't even think of it as a separate principle, because integrity is a central element that runs through all three of the other attributes. Without integrity everything else is meaningless. You never want anyone working for you who doesn't have impeccable integrity. We make a point of stressing how integrity is what we are all about.

So how do you know someone has integrity? It's hard to get good information on people today. References don't work very well. New laws have popped up. Employers have been sued when they report negative information regarding previous employment. That's why we actually give prospective associates an "integrity test," developed by Reid Psychological Systems, as part of the interview process. It's a series of yes or no and multiple choice questions, half dealing with drugs and alcohol and half with other matters that are revealing about a person's integrity. Some of the questions are fairly obvious, but there's a knack to how they're graded. The test asks things like: "If you could get into a movie without paying, and be sure you would not get caught, would you do it?" and "Do you believe a person who has taken money just a few times from the place where he works should be given another chance?"

Not everyone passes it, and of course there are other ways to probe into the issue of integrity, like the questioning we do during interviews. For instance, I always ask someone, "What are the four or five things you're most proud of?" I want them to blow their horn a little. Once they're through crowing about their children or their wife or their salesman of the month award, I'll say, "Anything you're not proud of?" I'm trying to determine if they're open enough to talk about things that might not make them comfortable. I'll notice how quickly they answer, and if they answer. If they simply say, "No, nothing," then that's a red flag that there might be an integrity issue.

We've tested this grid of four attributes again and again, and it seems to work.

Oh, by the way, it's not necessary but it really helps a lot if a prospective associate loves clothes, or whatever product it is you are selling.

Chapter 21

Now Enable Them

Hiring great people by these four standards gets you off to a terrific start. But their performance depends not only on these qualities. If you don't give them the right support and latitude, they'll stagnate.

The most important thing is that in our organization, everyone is *enabled*. A lot of businesses talk about empowering people, and that's the word we used as well. Nick Donofrio, Senior Vice President, Technology and Manufacturing, IBM Corporation, shared with me that the word empower might send the wrong message. Now, thanks to Nick, we believe enabling says it better than empowering.

Empowering allows the associate to do whatever it takes to make a customer extremely satisfied, but if an associate is enabled she knows she has the authority *plus* the resources to do it. The resources also provide a bit of structure, so that the enabled associate does not run amok. You are making it easier for them to succeed.

To us, the difference between enabling and empowering is the difference between delegation and abdication.

As I mentioned before, we have a non-hierarchical organization, and that's important if associates are going to feel enabled. Nobody brags about titles. Bill may be the vice chairman, but he'll never introduce himself that way. In fact, the title he puts on his business card is "coach." And we never refer to our people as employees. They're associates. Words, as I've said before, carry a lot of power. In many businesses, especially retail, I still hear the word "help." How would you like to be known as "the help" or "clerk"? Some associates like to call themselves consultants or personal shoppers, and that's fine. In one of Tom Peters's books, I recall, a woman on an assembly line says she is the "supreme commander," and that makes her feel better. All of our associates have business cards, because that says they're professionals.

Even brand-new associates know they are allowed to do *whatever it takes on the playing field* to exceed the customer's expectations. It's hard to hug if you're not free to make decisions. Emergencies come up on short notice; there's no time to go up some chain of command to seek approval. I want associates to trust their own instincts and just do what it takes.

Here's an example. A woman who is an executive at Pepsi called her sales associate one morning and said: "SOS! I have to go out of town on a business trip and I need a new outfit fitted." Lisa Iselin, without asking anyone, left the store and drove the twenty minutes to Pepsi's headquarters in Purchase, New York. The customer was in the boardroom, and she excused herself by saying: "I have something important to attend to." She had bought an outfit from us but hadn't had it fitted or tailored yet because she wanted to find the accessories for it first. But now she needed it that day. So she was fitted in her office, the outfit was taken back to the store to be altered, and then we returned it to her, that day.

Lisa didn't have to ask anyone if she could leave the store and do this, because she was enabled. She was doing whatever it took to please her customer.

Once a woman bought a pair of snow white pants from us. After one trip to the dry cleaners, they were the color of bone. She brought them in to Angela Guitard for advice. Angela said, "Here, let me have those. I'll take care of them for you." It was the dry cleaner's responsibility, but Angela, without asking anyone, gave the customer a credit for the pants and then, on her own, dealt with the dry cleaner, saving the customer the hassle.

But enabling doesn't mean to go haywire and not use any judgment. There's a famous story about how Nordstrom once took back a set of tires from a customer, even though it doesn't sell tires. Well, we pride ourselves on taking almost everything back, no questions asked, and with a smile. But we don't want our associates accepting dishwashers. You have to use your head.

Give your associates the freedom to make their own decisions, but don't forget to guide them.

Chapter 22

Cooperation versus Competition

No matter what business you're in, you always dream of landing a "big hitter," someone who buys a lot of your product, and does it month after month, year after year. Take my brother Bill. He gets his car washed practically every day. He's a car wash's dream. When a big hitter becomes a customer of ours, it's natural that intense competition develops among the associates to make that customer their own. And we encourage that. But the customer, not the associate, must make the final decision on who serves him. And everyone must accept that decision.

We think of this as cooperation versus competition.

Of course it's a downer for an associate who loses a big hitter, or any customer, to someone else. No one likes rejection. But that's what teamwork is all about. The business must be bigger than any individual ego.

Cooperation is really critical in the formula of success, because if associates don't build a positive and personal relationship with each other, the organization can become dysfunctional. And by the way, cooperation applies across job descriptions—buyers and shippers have to work with sellers too.

When someone comes into the store and doesn't ask for a particular seller, we educate our associates to ask the customer, "Do you normally work with someone?" If the answer, is, "Yes, Ray handles me," the associate finds Ray. If the answer is, "No," that customer is available for a relationship.

It is also fair game for associates to pursue customers who aren't getting the service they could get, or who might not have the right chemistry with their current associate. Sometimes a customer comes into the store and buys, but doesn't buy very much, because the associate serving him or her has let the relationship slip. Our associates Gail and Joe really built their business by taking a genuine interest in existing customers who didn't have close relationships with other associates. They asked the customers some open-ended questions, probed a little. Found out that they needed more dresses than they thought they did.

When Gail or Joe went to the computer system, they noticed that other sales associates were assigned to these particular customers. Each asked their colleagues, "How well do you know Sophia Potts or Lauren Kubik?" Often they barely knew them, and said they didn't mind if Gail or Joe took them on. So they changed the sales associate name in the computer to their own and went forward and often transformed those customers into big hitters. That's cooperation.

All the time, we run contests among the sales associates to keep their competitive juices flowing, but we also turn them into lessons in cooperation. For instance, whoever sells the most Zegna merchandise in a given period gets a trip to Europe. Some of our associates, however, have a lot more Zegna customers than others. To give everyone an equal shot at winning, we handicap the big sellers by subtracting some of their sales. It's sort of the way golfers level the playing field with handicaps. And the big sellers accept this. That's cooperation.

Our overall objective is to encourage associates to be competitive with *themselves* and with *other businesses*, but cooperative with fellow members of their team. Our managers set numerical goals and "stretch goals" for all of our associates (not just the sellers, but everyone), the stretch goals being difficult targets but ones we feel are attainable if the associates really work "smarter, not harder." This keeps the associates focused on improving their own performance without worrying about how anyone else is doing.

When you have cooperation among your associates, customers won't be confused about who services them but will bond with a particular associate, and that relationship becomes the reason for them to come into the store. All the time, we have customers who stop by for an emotional pickup, whether they buy something or not. They share their marital or business problems, or issues with their kids. The husband of one customer wrote his wife's associate a wonderful letter thanking her not just for helping her with her clothes but for helping her with her self-esteem. That sort of intimacy is why we think of ourselves as like the barber or hairdresser.

Many years ago, a customer who worked at Avon Products told me an actual barber story that I share with new associates. He religiously went to this barber in the Avon building in midtown Manhattan. But then one day the barber moved a few blocks away, into the New York Athletic Club. Now this man has less hair than I do, which is not a lot, but, would you believe, he walked those several blocks even though there were a number of other barbers still in the building that could have trimmed his hair. Why? Relationships. His barber gave him a hug every time he cut his hair. He told him a story and generally made him feel great.

Now, upon reflection, I would bet a nickel that if the manager or owner of that barber's old shop had said to this man, "Jim, we're sorry that Dan left, but I think Carlos knows you and he has watched how Dan cut your hair, and we would really love to continue to have your business, why don't you give Carlos an opportunity," then Jim might have given Carlos a shot.

And that's what we do when a sales associate leaves or dies, as one did, tragically, not long ago. We're unable to continue relationships into the afterlife, so I sent personal letters to his top clients. This action was followed up by our "Carloses," who later called them to see if they could begin a new relationship. Relationships, of course, can be with stores, barbershops, beauty salons, banks, brokerage firms, or car dealers.

If an associate is unable to establish positive relationships with peers, then he or she has to go. There are two reasons why someone doesn't work out: They don't "get" the culture, or they don't want to get it. If someone doesn't get it, we work with the associate and give the person second and even third chances. But if the associate refuses to do it—and we haven't had many of those—then the person has to go, and immediately.

In a hugging culture, if everyone cooperates, then the business as a whole becomes a winner. If everyone gets this, then individual egos rarely get out of control. As Bruce Kelly, our superstar shoe seller, said, "You don't care if you're batting ninth if it's for the Yankees, because the Yankees are winners. It's the same way in business. We have sellers who would be Number 1 at any other store and they're Number 11 here. And we all feel like world champions." Sales associates come to us and they stay. They think career, and even though each is always a free agent, they don't want to be traded.

Chapter 23

Training Is for Dogs, Education Is for People

Life is a matter of continuous learning, and yet most businesses, particularly small businesses, don't do enough to educate their associates. Frankly, we need to do a lot more too. We need to raise the bar for all of our associates, including me. Too many businesses think education is overly expensive and only for big corporations. Well, it doesn't have to be costly. By the way, we don't like the word "train." The way we look at it, you train dogs, and you educate people.

We loosely maintain the "Mitchells/Richards University," a sort of orientation program involving tapes, especially those of Michael Yacobian, that teach how to engage a customer, and how to talk to customers and turn them into loyal clients. We educate our team with FranklinCovey's method of time management. It's hard to believe, but many associates come to us and they don't even own a calendar. We actually have to educate them that they need one to write down appointments, both professional and personal. You don't need a calendar to sell something today, but you do need one for a relationship for tomorrow and beyond. We talk about the store history, the vision, the mission, and guiding principles.

But the most important parts of our education are informal. The everyday meetings that include product knowledge, usually given by the buyers, independently or in conjunction with our vendors—someone from Zegna, Hermès, Armani, or Hickey-Freeman—who share with us what's new for the season, or how to order or reorder more effectively. Many mornings we stand around in an informal meeting and share with each other service stories of what happened the day before. We also take our associates on bus or train trips to the New York showrooms, where they listen to representatives from the various manufacturers. The meetings and sharing of these stories create a special type of bonding that is fostered by a hugging, sharing culture.

One of the things that surprises us a lot is how little other businesses bother to master what their product is all about. You walk into an electronics store looking for a DVD player and there are about eighty different ones on the wall. You tell the salesman your needs and ask him what's the best model? Ninety-nine percent of the time, it seems, he'll scratch his head and say, "Well, we've got a special sale on this Beat-All-Else model over here." The guy has no clue about you and your desires, or is it for your grandson Bob or your granddaughter Kathleen? We see this all the time, in business after business.

When we think of all the things we pass on to our new associates, these are the five most important ones we really want them to learn:

1. **Think customers first! It's a mindset. Visualize them as empress and emperor!** From the minute you wake up until the minute you go to bed, and in your dreams too, you have to think customers. Nothing is more important in a hugging culture. The customer has to be the center of the universe, the empress or the emperor.

   One of our people used to begin every day by touring the store and straightening up the merchandise. He checked that the floor was clean of litter, that there were no lightbulbs out, that every display was just so. He was very focused on "housekeeping."

   I asked him once, "What's the first thing you think of in the morning?" He said straight back, "That everything in the store is neat." I just shook my head. "The first thought has to be the customers. Think customers. How the store looks is important, but the most important thing is the customers." As a little aid, I told him that he had to go a week and not once straighten a piece of merchandise, no matter how messy anything was. Believe me, he had a torturous week. It was a hard habit to break. Today he thinks of customers while straightening the stock.

2. **Engage . . . with warmth.** We encourage associates to engage with customers in a friendly, smiling, personal manner. Everyone ought to have a smile on his or her face. When you meet someone and the person smiles, you feel warmer. A customer said just the other day, "Why is everyone in here smiling? I am really beginning to feel good. Frankly, come to think of it, I'm feeling great!"

Associates should even smile when they talk on the phone. Most people don't know this, but when you smile it actually changes your intonation and makes you sound cheerier. There's a real estate firm that actually puts a little mirror on their phones so their agents can check that they're smiling while they're talking.

When speaking to a customer in person, eye contact is very important. We kid associates when we try to emphasize this: "Do you know the color of your top customers' eyes?" Think about it with your own friends. Some people don't know the color of their son-in-law's or daughter-in-law's eyes. It's a hugging game for all of us to try.

As I said before, if you're going to engage people, use first names. We're very open in telling our associates that the purpose is to bring sales associates up to the level of professionalism with the customer. Many times it sends a clear message to the customer that we are open for intimacy and trust. I'll bet a pound that George Bush called Tony Blair, "Tony," and Tony called George Bush, "George," the first time they shook hands. They wanted to trust each other.

Now and then, we've had associates who have had a hard time coming around to that way of thinking. Anne Marie, in particular, just couldn't bring herself to do it. She came to America as an au pair from Norway, and her upbringing had taught her that it was respectful to call someone Mr. or Mrs. or Ms., not Michael or Jill. I coached her and gently nudged her over the hump. I told her, "You need to make the switch. You'll find it will make a big difference. I'm not going to fire you or anything if you don't use first names, but I'd really be happy if you'd give it a try. Remember, you're a professional. Your customers are relying on you to dress them for the ball and for their jobs. You're important to them." I said, "You don't open your front door and welcome your friend by saying, 'Come on in, Mrs. O'Connor.' You say, 'Claire, great to see you, come on in.' " Well, she started doing it and before long had completed the switch. She went from selling a half million dollars' worth of clothing a year to selling a million dollars. Maybe it wasn't just the name switch, but it didn't hurt.

Many years ago we actually retained an expert to help us memorize names. I even remember his name, Lou Weinstein. He taught us tricks like associating the name with something else—for example "Smith" with "blacksmith"—and repeating the name as often as possible while speaking to the person.

Another thing is, never, ever should an associate say, "May I help you?" A customer hears that and immediately feels pressured to buy something. And says, "No, just looking." Instead, associates should ask about the customer, not the product.

Always finish the sale with a common courtesy "thank-you." That thank-you is how we feel, so we might as well say it. It's genuine. How many times have you made an important purchase—maybe even spent a lot of money on clothes, cars, or an expensive bottle of wine—and no one even thanked you? I try always to look a client in the eye and say, "Thank you for your business!" It is received as a big hug.

3. **Profile, profile, profile.** As I mentioned in Hugging 101, we urge associates to ask customers open-ended questions about themselves, on the three aspects of their lives: business, personal, and family. We want to know why they need a dress or pantyhose rather than just showing them to the size 8s or the pantyhose rack. This allows us to build a profile of the customers, which is the foundation for a relationship. We want to know their convictions, their proudest moments, their values, whether they collect dog license tags or toothpick holders, whatever allows us to really understand them.

This is part of what we call the Client Accumulation Program (inspired by Michael Yacobian), the way in which you build a relationship, in order to turn a customer into a loyal one who returns again and again. In the next chapter, on technology, I'll go into detail about exactly what we mean by "client," and how we store and use the information we gather to serve clients beyond their expectations, every visit.

When we hire new associates, we also ask them to tell us things about themselves from the Business, Personal, and Family categories. It helps us learn more about them, but what we're also doing is preparing them to profile customers. It demonstrates to them how easy it is to gather information about others. You don't have to pry, you just have to be interested and probe a little. We find that the easy way to get started is with small talk, and then to ask, "How's business?" or "How's your family?" People love to talk about their work and their family, and that opens the door. And turn your questions into conversation. "Oh, you have a ten-year-old daughter? My girl's the same age. She just started playing the tuba.

What's your daughter interested in?" And the relationship builds.

4. **Use common sense.** I know this sounds too obvious even to mention, but if it's so obvious, why is it so routinely ignored? It's one of the foundation bricks of good service. Bill likes to tell new associates this little story. His son Scott was a freshman at Dartmouth, and it was Parents' Weekend. They were sitting in Scott's economics class. The professor was talking about the various strategies of some cottage industries. He had a blizzard of formulas covering the blackboard and a stack of case studies. At the end, he threw the studies on the floor, erased all the formulas, and asked, "OK, what are the two words that are most germane to this class?" Scott raised his hand and said, "Cash flow." That wasn't it. Bill stuck up his hand and suggested, "Thank you." The professor thanked him, but said that was wrong. Someone else tried, "Yes, please." Nobody had the right answer. It was "common sense." Bill commented, "Nobody got it that day, and I am still amazed when I go shopping elsewhere, very few ever seem to get it. So much reduces to common sense."

One afternoon a woman brought in a dress in one of our boxes. The dress had moth holes in it. I hesitated because, first of all, the dress was a size 8 and the woman was a size 14, and second, I knew that the dress was at least three years old. The computer said four years. When we asked a few questions, the truth came out. She was a maid, and she found the dress in the closet of the woman she had worked for, who had recently died. Fair is fair, and that wasn't fair. We wouldn't take it back. "Okay," she said, and we had a cup of coffee together and reminisced about her former employer, who had been a great customer of ours.

5. **The three E's.** To hug effectively, there are three E's: Energy, Enthusiasm, and Execution. Add them together and they equal excellence. Some people think it's enough to have energy and enthusiasm. Hardly. In fact, it doesn't matter how much you have of those two traits if you don't execute. In the great huggers, you see all three. They have an abundance of the first two traits, but where they really distinguish themselves is by the third. They execute. They're always focusing on executing the current sale and quickly setting up the next step.

How often have you bought something, and a couple of weeks later the person who sold it to you called to see how you liked it? My guess would be just about never. When you bought your last dishwasher, did the appliance salesman call to see how the dishes were doing? When you bought a house, did the real estate agent even bother to check back and make sure you hadn't discovered termites or quicksand in the backyard?

Well, we try to call every customer after their clothing is altered and delivered to make sure they are extremely satisfied with their alterations and their shopping experience. We call these satisfaction calls. It's a hug. And you might get one if all you bought was a tie. That's executing.

Executing is selling a customer everything they need or desire, not just settling for the quick hit. Making the complete sale is what a relationship is all about. Linda and I always hate it when we've gone shopping for toys for our seven grand-children, and the salesperson sells us a firetruck or an airplane and doesn't bother to tell us that it needs batteries, and they're not included. Or they sell us C batteries and the truck needs AA. Then, on Christmas morning, when one of our grand-children is eager to play with their new firetruck, I've got to go driving all over town looking for a place that's open and carries batteries.

In our business, the point was made very effectively, and very visually, by Joanne, who was our store manager in the early 1980s. Early on a Saturday morning, in front of the entire staff—all the sellers, the tailors, everyone—she stood up wear-ing only a three-piece men's suit. No blouse, no shoes, no socks, no belt.

"This is the way you guys sold my father his new suit," she said. "Now you have to understand, he's a big-shot executive who gets up early in the morning, while my mother is asleep on the other side of the bed, and he uses a flashlight to look for a shirt and tie that will go with the suit. He couldn't find anything to match, and he's ticked off at me and my mom and Mitchells! And you guys think it's great, because you sold him a $795 suit." Everyone quickly got the point.

That's why we always urge new associates to watch other great sellers sell. They have been doing it for so long, I say they are playing from their inner game. Everybody has a different style and way in which they play the game. Tiger Woods's swing is very different from

Arnold Palmer's. The idea is to first have some fundamentals and then what you say and how you close and how you follow through are individual. Watching the great sellers gives you ideas to incorporate and make your own.

Remember, a well-educated associate is an effective associate.

Chapter 24

Now Care for Them

Hiring, enabling, and educating great people is half the job. You also have to do everything possible to keep them. That means you've got to care for them, and care for them regularly.

After all, if the associates are not "up" and they don't look forward to coming to work, how are they going to go that extra step for the customer? Contrary to conventional wisdom, it's not just about money or commissions. It's a combination of factors why our associates work with us. The hugging working environment, the little things you do for them, and the prestige of the store in the community rank up there with compensation considerations.

We believe there are four key ways to care for associates and keep them happy.

1. **Pay them well.** While it's not just about money, everyone does have bills to pay. We believe in paying people well. In the end, they'll be more than worth it. Russell came up with the terrific idea of adding extra percentages to the commission we pay at Mitchells for certain levels that an associate sells over a million dollars. This program was actually instituted before there were any million-dollar sellers. The point is to really put our money on the table for "high impact" sellers. The way we see it, they earn it.

   Interestingly, when we bought Richards the sales associates there were paid straight salary. We pay commission to most sellers at Mitchells, because we feel that it is the best way to reward them. But they were used to straight salary at Richards, and didn't want to change. So we agreed to keep the system as it was, for new hires as well. It made them feel enabled that we went with what they wanted. And you know what? The associates at Richards sell just as effectively as the associates at Mitchells, even though that goes completely against conventional wisdom in our industry.

2. **Give them a life**. One crucial way we care for our associates is by the hours we keep. The hours of a seller, no matter what they sell, can be brutal and not leave much time for anything else. A lot of stores, especially those in malls, are open late several nights a week and also during the day on Sunday. Some car dealerships stay open Sundays, trying to get an edge. We are not open Sunday (except during the holiday season), and are only open Thursday night. That's because forcing our associates to work that much would disrupt, if not destroy, the

hugging relationship we have with them, and then they would not be motivated to build a hugging relationship with their customers and clients.

Many associates at other stores work an erratic schedule of fifty hours or more a week, and have no time for any life beyond suits and dresses. Our associates have a life.

It might appear to a customer (especially a new one) that our hours go against ideal customer service, because customers sometimes want to shop late and on Sundays. But we have built our business on relationships—relationships between our associates and customers—and customers know we will open early in the morning, stay late at night, and, if they have an emergency, come in on Sunday. But to attract and retain great associates you need to allow them balance between work and the rest of their lives. Many businesses don't foster that balance, and that's why many have mediocre associates. On the one hand, we might do more business initially if we were open Sundays and additional evenings, but on the other hand, it doesn't feel right for the long run because it's the antithesis of our culture.

And when it comes to hours, we allow for individual quirks. One of our associates, who is sixty-four and going strong, knew us well enough to "confess" that he tended to get very tired during the selling day and would sneak away for an hour or so and take a nap in his car. I told him that was terrific, that he knew his chemistry and his body well enough to pace himself, and mentioned that I often did that myself. Big shots call it a power nap, and I told him he was a big shot, too.

3. **Know their hot buttons.** Just as we ask our sales associates to SKU their customers and know as much or more about them as they know about our product, we ask our managers, including me, to SKU our associates and learn as much or more about them as we know about our customers. (Remember, SKU means stock keeping unit.) This allows us to stay close to their hot buttons.

For instance, we're big on saying the right words. Take Bill. You have to say "good morning" to him the first time you see him every morning or he thinks there is something wrong. He's just sensitive about that, as are many people. That's one of his hot buttons. On the other hand, if I constantly say good morning to a more introverted person, they may feel imposed upon. I breeze past a lot of people in the morning and fail to say anything to them, because I've got something else on my mind. But I've programmed myself to say good morning to Bill, no matter what else is going on, because that matters to him.

Some employees like to be called on their birthdays, or to get a card. Or they like to get a kind note on each anniversary with us: "Congratulations on your sixth anniversary working for us. Let's make it sixty more." Something like that. Others couldn't care less, but the trick is to know what employees care about and then respond in kind.

I love to tell the Heidi Williams flower story. Years ago, we were interviewing Heidi for our team. She finally said she would join us, and we were thrilled. We could sense it was a big decision for her, because she is a very loyal and committed person who had established relationships at Macy's. So we sent her flowers with a handwritten note welcoming her to Mitchells and telling her how bright her future was here.

A couple of years after she joined us, we were in a group seminar talking about hugging and relationship selling, and Heidi shared the flower story and revealed something we never knew. She said that after agreeing to join us, Macy's had made her a counter offer, and she told them she would think about it. Driving home, she had mixed feelings, but when she got to her house and saw the flowers and read my personalized note welcoming her aboard, that touched her. Most people think a hot button is something big, but it can also be incredibly small, like a bouquet of flowers and a nice note.

4. **Treat them to something special.** Another effective way to care for associates is to surprise them with a treat. How about lunch in Rome? We took Rita Roman, our first million-dollar seller, and her husband, Mark, to Italy, and we did the same thing with Frank Gallagi and Pat, his wife. When Bob Mitchell was looking to acquire some expertise in private-label tailoring, he took Tullio Giannitti Sr., our master tailor at Richards, to Italy. There aren't many retailers that bring sellers or tailors along on trips. Believe me, they loved it.

Domenic Condoleo, our head tailor in Westport, loves soccer, so when the World Cup was played in the United States, Bill Mitchell took Dom to all of the games. Not only in New York, but also in Boston and Los Angeles.

Jeff Kozak loves the Mets, and since a number of Jeff's customers have box seats at Shea Stadium, he gets invited to a lot of Mets games, and he always goes to Opening Day, even if it's Saturday. We're fine about that, because it's one special way we hug him.

We also use this approach on sick calls. Many bosses visit ill associates in the hospital (though try to remember the last time your boss visited you when you were laid up), and we do too. But we try to take it to the next level and do something special that surprises them.

Some years ago, Mel Gross, one of our senior buyers, got very sick. I used to kid him that he was the only associate that we permitted to be negative (believe me, it was always partly cloudy with Mel, but his weak heart was a heart of gold). He had a couple of bypasses, and on top of that a gallbladder removed, and next to the family I was the first one to see him. I really wanted to show how much I cared about him, so I snuck in with fresh-squeezed orange juice and tiramisu that Linda made for him. He liked to kid that his wife, Fran, always made him fresh-squeezed orange juice, that it was in the contract, and he adored tiramisu.

If you demonstrate how much you care about your associates that, in turn, will cause them to care about their customers. Everyone wins.

HUGGING STUDY GUIDE #3

People/Service/Product—service must come before product, but the great people who work for you come first, because you don't give service in a vacuum.

Four qualities make a great associate—they must be *competent and confident,* they must have a *positive attitude,* and they must have a *passion to listen, learn, and grow* to be their best. Finally, *integrity,* in the broadest sense, must run through all of these attributes.

Enable, don't just empower associates—hugging works best when people have great latitude to do whatever it takes within the boundaries of the business, but they are expected to seek guidance when they're unsure of themselves or need coaching to grow.

Cooperation versus competition—if associates don't build positive and personal relationships with one another, the organization can become dysfunctional.

Educate, don't train—most of all, associates must learn to place the customer first, engage with warmth, use common sense, profile customers, and embrace the Three E's. When you combine Energy + Enthusiasm + Execution, you achieve Excellence.

Care for your associates—you can't expect them to hug customers if you don't show you care for them: Pay them well, give them a life, know their hot buttons, and surprise them with perks that are special for them.

Olive Doesn't Work Here Anymore

You Can't Compete without Technology

PART FOUR

Clive Doesn't Work
Here Anymore

Chapter 25

Technology Must
Support Hugging

Our parents started with the idea that they would offer wonderful service and know all about each customer. In the early days, Dad could pretty much keep his customers' needs stored in his head. But as the business grew, we noticed we were increasingly reliant on a wonderful and energetic woman named Olive. She did all the accounts receivable on a rickety old machine and kept information on customers on scraps of paper. We thought the world of Olive, but this system struck us as a little hairy. What if something happened to Olive? What if something happened to those pieces of paper?

We needed to automate. After all, managers have to give their associates tools for effective hugging, and we realized that the best tool of all is technology. Technology, it was obvious to us, is the backbone of any modern successful company. Two businesses can be equal in every possible way, but if one has great technology and the other doesn't, the one without the technology can't possibly keep up.

We realized early on that technology not only tells you how you're doing, but it collects accurate customer data that you can use for more precisely targeted, more efficient marketing efforts. Technology enables you to anticipate your customers' wishes before they know them themselves. And technology allows you to speak to customers in a common voice throughout the organization. Technology is a million Olives rolled into one.

So, as we thought about our dependence on Olive and how Olive would get old and retire and enjoy her golden years and not work for us anymore, we decided we had to incorporate technology into the customer-service vision established by Dad. We had to go high-tech and never look back.

The critical thing about technology is, it must support hugging. Since we're all about understanding our customers' needs, preferences, and buying patterns, the technology had to be designed to help do that. What's amazing is that although personal relationships are absolutely crucial to any company's success, they are rarely tracked by any system. Hotels don't know who likes queen-size beds and who wants extra pillows. Airlines don't know who prefers aisle seats and who prefers the window.

It was in the early seventies that we made the decision to computerize Mitchells. At that time, this was unheard of for a business of our size, but we strongly believed it had to be done if we were to live up to our full potential and fulfill the vision to dominate our market. Right from the beginning, we decided to go with "Big Blue." After all, we already had a lot of IBM customers, and technology in the early 1970s to a Chinese history major who had been raising money and doing accounting at a research institute added up to IBM.

We began our relationship with IBM back in 1972, and we went through a succession of machines until we finally purchased the IBM AS/400 that we use to this day. It's a powerful midsize computer that we connected to terminals on the sales floor, throughout the organization, and online at home. Looking back, it's quite clear that it was one of the smartest moves we ever made. Incidentally, Scott Willard, the IBM salesman who sold us our first computer, went on to start his own software company and comes to us to buy his clothes. Now we use the system he sold us to serve him. Full circle hug!

Once we had the hardware, we took the next step, which was to install comprehensive Customer Relationship and Point of Sale software. While we bought the initial guts of the software from a company associated with IBM, Russ and Todd customized it with Sara Lee, our programmer in California. We designed our system to keep the mom-and-pop, stay-close-to-the-customer philosophy while serving tens of thousands of customers. Plus, it's integrated so that all of the accounting, marketing, merchandising, and sales data tie into each other. You don't have to go to two or three places to get the reports, as is true in many systems.

One of the things that's made a big difference is that we always have been in control of our technology. It always has been in-house. Other systems that are on the market are designed by computer companies, not by retailers. Almost every business buys software and then has to adapt the business to the software. We did the opposite. We tailored the software around our business principles and operations. Technology works best if it's highly customized to your business.

Our technology truly is simple to use. We feel that's important. Too many businesses have such complex technology that the senior executives have no idea how to use it, so they don't even bother trying. We think it is critically important that the CEO not only support technology, but also can use all the systems; so our technology was designed so that even someone like me, a proud grandfather now, who's still working on how to program a VCR, can understand it.

It takes a lot of effort, and it's a major initial investment to install the technology system that's right for your business. But once it's up and running, you can't help but improve customer service. We had a sales associate who came to us from a New York competitor, and when he gave notice, the owner tried to persuade him to stay. The associate told him, "They've got all sorts of new things going there. They've got computers that track customers." The owner tried to insist that his business was doing a lot of fabulous new things too, until the associate asked, "What have you done recently?" And he said, "Well, we just remodeled our store and got a new carpet."

Don't sit around putting in new carpeting while your sales associates, or for that matter your customers, desert you for a place that knows how to use technology. Just keep in mind that the technology must support hugging and enhance the relationship.

Chapter 26

We Know You,
Plus Your Favorite Necktie

In 1990, Russ and I were attending a meeting of retailers in Carmel, California. We were scanning our inventory reports, looking at our watches because we wanted to escape to the links at Pebble Beach. The next speaker, who was addressing the group on extraordinary customer service, put his finger in our face and said, "Do you guys know as much about your customers as you do about your inventory?" And we paused and said, "Honestly, no."

Boom. Lightning struck. We had a handshake and a high five and we agreed that we would design our entire system around the customers first, because clearly our culture called for it.

Most of the technology systems you see are focused on inventory, on the allocation of product between stores, as well as on banking and financial issues—and that's important stuff. In the majority of cases, however, the systems largely ignore the client base of the organization.

The really important difference between our system and those at other businesses is that we know every item that every customer buys and a lot about who that customer is. As important, we know what customers did not buy. Every man and woman wears shoes. So if we notice that a customer is buying a lot of clothes from us and not buying shoes, that means the person is going somewhere else for them and we need to encourage them to break that habit.

Most companies layer customers into their IT systems after all the product information is set into place. We layer the customers first. It's a mindset. Everything else follows. What this allows us to do, literally, is turn our customers into SKUs, or stock keeping units. I told you how our sales associates gather personal information as they help their customers make their purchases. Well, that allows us to punch some buttons and call up a customer, and the screen tells us where they live and work. We see their spouses' names and their kids' names. We see their birthday and anniversary. We see if they like to be called Mrs. or Ms. And since we treat customers as family, we ought to know their nicknames: Elizabeth is Corky, Anthony is Tony, Theresa is Tracy, Dorothy is Dot, Victor is Vic, Weston is Wes. And, of course, we see their sizes and favorite colors.

On top of this, all the details of what they've bought and when they bought it go into the system, where they can be retrieved at a moment's notice. We see how their buying habits trend, how long they wait to come pick up finished alterations, and we can also tell if they buy anything when they do come in to pick something up. Most retailers can't tell you the details of their top fifty customers. All they can do is make an educated guess, because they don't track every type of sale. Or the data is not integrated with all of their stores. They may track their own credit cards or their house accounts, but maybe not

MasterCard or American Express, or maybe not, God love the customer, cash.

It's important to understand why customers buy and why they don't buy. With the click of a button, a sales associate with a password can instantly see a customer's complete buying history. Another private screen contains notes that the sales associate has entered into the profile, such as marriage, divorce, promotion, geographic relocation, a new child, a pet—factors that help the associate recall personal information that enhances the hugging relationship.

The first question people ask me when they hear about our technology system is how do we get the information? It's a very simple answer. We just ask! As I discussed earlier, one of the most important things we educate our associates about is how to profile customers by gently asking questions. Of course the customers have to be in a reasonable hugging environment so they trust you and feel you will use the information to serve them better.

To encourage our associates to do these profiles, we get a report every day on how many customers each associate has profiled, and so does each associate. Anybody below the average in profiling his or her customers has got to get "back to school" and work with me or our managers on how she can improve her profiling abilities.

Once the information goes into the computer, it doesn't go away. Most companies purge the data they collect on customers after a year or two. We save it. It's like gold—actually, in some cases better than gold. Like platinum. For instance, we have every single sale to every single customer at Mitchells since 1989 and at Richards since May 1996, six months after we acquired the store.

Naturally, it's also extremely important that we protect the sanctity of this information, and we make sure we do. We never share it with anyone, and unlike some other stores, we never sell our list to others for big bucks. We would never even think of doing that. And customers trust us.

Our customers know that we have all of this data, and that we can use it for their benefit. This knowledge bonds them to us in a very powerful way and creates loyalty.

We've heard many stories similar to this customer's: "Oh, I was in Paris last week and had an hour to kill, and I went into this fancy designer store and tried on a half dozen beautiful outfits, and this saleslady kept saying, 'Darling, you look just beautiful!' in every single one, and I knew I didn't. All of a sudden, I asked myself, What am I doing? Susie Burian knows me, she knows my taste, and she knows my body. And here I am today, and I bought three new outfits and I love them and I love her."

Chapter 27

It's How You Use It—
Your Mindset

All businesses gather data of one sort or another. But the important thing is how that data gets used, and how you execute.

Whenever I go to the grocery store, I always feel lost. They always seem to be shuffling things around, and I feel like I'm on a scavenger hunt. What's more, even when I make a list I always forget something. Imagine if you went into a supermarket, and they SKU'd their customers like we do on every item in the store—sausage, milk, cheese, cereal, chicken cutlets—and they gave you a handheld device specific to the store. You could dictate your shopping list to the person at the customer service desk, and he could type it in. Out would come a printed list telling you what aisle each item is in—the shelf, the price, the works. In addition, by searching through your previous purchases, they could make some recommendations. Say you normally buy ketchup once a month and it's been a month. The handheld device would suggest you might be running low, maybe you'd better pick up a bottle. They've got a special on pineapples, and they know you're a sucker for pineapples, so the device would point that out, and of course you would grab a few.

You can taste them already.

This is what we try to do with our information. The best use of it is for an appointment. You can plan and prepare. But sometimes a customer just walks in the door, and the sales associate often quickly punches the customer's name into the computer and up comes the person's profile. The associate scans the information, refreshing her memory about the customer's likes and dislikes. If she sees that the customer loves cappuccino, she'll get her a cappuccino. If she sees she has a weakness for M&M's, she'll offer her a handful.

She'll take note of the customer's sizes and price points. If she sees that the customer never spends more than $750 on a dress, she's not going to show her one for $1,000, unless she has the sense that the person is ready to take the plunge to a new level. When someone comes in and announces she was just made the chief financial officer of her company, after being the assistant CFO, the associate would congratulate her and suggest she might want to go to the next level of dress quality.

Some customers want to cruise around. They don't want to have a dialogue. That goes into the profile. Some like delivery. Some like to be called; some don't. By the way, we never, ever make a cold call. We ask permission. That goes for mail as well. There is even a place where we can indicate "no mail." We have to know these preferences if we're going to deliver extraordinary personal service. The mindset has to be that every customer is unique and wants different things.

Our system enables us to anticipate needs. When it's slow on the floor, an effective sales associate, like Richard or Joe, will sift through his database. He'll notice that his good customer, Mike, likes light beige Abboud suits, and one just came in. He'll give him a call and see if he wants to stop by and take a look at it. Because we service a lot of people who are very busy, we can turn our knowledge into time efficiencies, which is critical to our client base.

The quantity of data we track allows us to know more than most vendors and suppliers do about what is and what isn't selling to whom. What happens is, vendors depend on us to forecast trends in the industry *for them*. And we are able to order more accurately rather than simply follow general vendor suggestions that don't necessarily apply to our target audience. This is a big hug relationship builder between us!

Another thing technology does is help us understand trends and large-scale behavior. Businesses often make assumptions based on sketchy, anecdotal evidence that may be misleading. We like to say, "What you don't know can hurt you." Everyone always told us that women are "never" loyal, they shop in five to ten stores. But we looked at our own research and found that our women customers are, in many individual cases, more loyal than men—it's the personal relationship with the business and the sales associate that produces loyalty. That convinced us to make sure we service all the needs of our women customers, not assume that if they rarely buy a sweater from us it is because they get their sweaters at another store they frequent and there is no way we can get all of their business.

Our system also defines the performance of every associate—the number of clients and customers, the average sale, and the average return. Sometimes, of course, we use this information to measure an associate's performance. But mostly we use it to help the associates learn how to improve their game.

We have a grid for sellers that includes number of customers each day, average sale, average returns, and of course the dollars. Obviously, if an associate doesn't know some of these numbers, she doesn't know how she's doing, so we do share the various important numbers based on these factors in this grid. Essentially, the more customers you have and the more frequently they come in, the more business you will do. And if you wait on twenty customers a day and your average sale is $100, or someone has ten customers a day and the average sale is $1,000, you say to the first associate, "Raise your average sale," and to the second associate, "Wait on more customers without sacrificing the average sale." It sounds simple, but to execute it takes time and it takes building a relationship with an associate so they trust you that you are not trying to beat them up but are trying to enable them to have fun, to grow, and to sell more.

Take the case of one of our associates, who had been working at Macy's and really didn't have a long career in retail before we hired her at Mitchells. When I reviewed all of her statistics, like a manager would size up a player, her average sale was lower than others. When I dug into it, I realized that she just couldn't bring herself to sell a woman a $250 blouse or a $350 pair of pants. Her attitude was, "Who would ever buy something that expensive?" But thank God many customers do. We said to her, "Wouldn't you rather have them buy it from you than go to Barneys or Bergdorf's? Just take a deep breath and try it. If you believe that she looks great in it, and you know she can afford it, say to Joyce, 'Buy it, you'll look fabulous. And don't you feel just great!' " Eventually, our associate did just that. In time, she got more and more confident, and her sales skyrocketed.

Technology also enables you to perform some detective work. That's exactly what we did when a customer filed a missing-suit complaint.

As I mentioned earlier, if anyone calls the store after hours, the call is forwarded to Bill's house. If he's not in, the call goes to Todd's house, and then to Andrew's, so a Mitchell is available no matter what the time. One Sunday night, a call came into the store, went to Bill, who was out, and then to Todd, who picked it up. One of our customers was at a hotel in Washington. The next morning, he was expected at the White House. He had just taken his clothes out of his Mitchells travel bag and was alarmed. He was a 46 Long. The suit in the bag was a 38 Short.

Here's what he figured happened. When he went to store his Mitchells travel bag in the airplane's hanging garment area, he had noticed another identical suit bag. Apparently, the other man mistakenly took his bag and he had his. Was there any way to track down his suit? There was, thanks to IBM and the Russ Mitchell computer system. Todd logged on to his home computer and went into our database. He sorted out customers of ours who wore 38 Short. Bingo! Only one name stood out. Todd called, and the man's wife said, yes, her husband was in Washington, and gave Todd the name of the hotel. Todd called and arranged for the men to switch bags and everyone was extremely happy—a huge hug.

For sure, this couldn't have been accomplished with Olive and her pieces of paper.

Chapter 28

Having Just Enough Product

Having too much inventory is very costly and can ruin your business fast. On the other hand, if you have too little inventory, you risk being out of stock when customers want something. If someone comes in looking for a size 4 or 14 in a new dress, and you don't have it, no matter how great your service is, you're not going to make a sale, and more important, you risk losing a loyal customer. That's why an important aspect of our system is how it helps us manage our product.

I'll never forget the woman who was dying to tell me this story when she learned I was one of the owners of Richards: She had been shopping at one of our competitors looking for a dress for a bat mitzvah. "Now," she said, "you can see I'm a twelve up top and probably a dash more on the bottom. [I could see she was at least a 16.] And when nobody approached me or tried to help me, I went right up to a sales associate, and said, 'Why don't you have my size in these nice

dresses? All I could find were twos, fours, and maybe some sixes.' "
The sales associate told her, "To be honest with you, ma'am, you're
not the customer profile we're looking for." On top of not serving her,
they insulted her.

So I told her, "We love real people, not profiles." I turned her over
to Belinda at Richards, who found the perfect sizes for her, and Sylvia
fitted her. She left as happy as a clam!

We can do this, because the customized reports we generate allow
us to accurately manage inventory, minimize shrinkage, respond
quickly to market trends, and execute more effectively. Whenever our
inventory gets out of whack, our technology enables us to make quick
professional judgments. This is really important during difficult economic times. We've been able to move from the old mentality of "the
more you buy, the more you sell" to the current buying philosophy of
having the right merchandise at the right time at the right price. We're
able to get reports on inventory management by vendor, by classification, by size, and by division. We get data on turn rate, mark-on
percentages, gross margins. All of these reports, like the customer reports, can be produced daily for the buyers and anyone else who is
interested in them.

We want to know things like what percentage of our new customers return within one year. And we want to know why new customers
didn't return. Was it because we didn't have enough selection in their
size, or was it something else? One of our strategies is to try to reac-
tivate customers.

Valbella, one of my favorite Greenwich restaurants, keeps track of
the wines its important customers like, and makes sure it has those
bottles on hand for whenever those customers come in to dine.

You just never know what information you'll need, and how it can help you hug. Suzanna, a longtime customer of ours, came in one day absolutely devastated. "Thank God no one was hurt," she said, "but our house burned down and my husband and I lost all of our clothes other than what we had on." We immediately extended our sympathies and took care of her immediate needs. Then we went to the computer, hit some buttons, and instantly pulled up a record of everything they had bought. It took a minute or two to print out and we gave it to her. The printout was invaluable for her insurance claim, and it also enabled us to help them replace their wardrobe. A real hug. We later learned that even the insurance company was thrilled.

The right technology means the right inventory.

Chapter 29

Climbing the Pyramid

Our sales associates move a lot of merchandise. We have thirty associates who sell $1 million a year, five who sell more than $2 million, and our wonder woman, Phyllis Bershaw, who sells more than $3 million. The million-dollar seller is a big number in our business, and it wasn't that long ago that that was considered an unattainable number. We expect new sales associates to sell that much during their first year.

You rack up those big numbers by building a relationship with everyone who comes in the door. Every associate has a story about some rumpled guy who stumbled in to buy a bow tie and left with several thousand dollars' worth of merchandise.

But while we do everything imaginable for anyone who walks into our store, including someone who spends fifty dollars a year and only buys socks, if you're going to really drive the business and grow the business, you have to pay particular attention to your biggest customers.

There's a classic business axiom that says that 20 percent of your customers account for 80 percent of your business, and it's true, of course, with us. So if you think of the entire customer base as a pyramid, the top of the pyramid represents the 20 percent that accounts for 80 percent of our business, and the vast 80 percent of the customers that produce 20 percent of sales forms the foundation. We instruct our associates to use our technology to focus a little extra on the top of the pyramid without ever neglecting the bottom.

We felt we needed to dig in and learn more about these top-of-the-pyramid customers, so we developed our own benchmark to classify them (you can define yours in your business), which is that they've spent at least $5,000 in a twelve-month period during any of the last three years. Some of them spend tens of thousands of dollars. Internally, we refer to these people as "clients." We designate each one in our system as a client, provided the sales associate knows him well enough to recognize him with a "Hi, Jerry!" and enters key profile data on them.

Here's a simple equation that we have found works: *A customer plus a relationship plus a benchmark equals a client.* Of course every business will have its own benchmark, and when you uncover the needs of a customer you create a client.

Sales associates get monthly reports showing the activity of their clients so they can study their shopping patterns, seeing what they're buying, what they're not buying, and how frequently they're buying with us. We want the associates to be sure they're serving their clients' needs, hugging them, and exceeding their expectations.

Bruce, one of our associates, is an interesting study. He was a totally transactional seller who took a while for the lightbulb to go on. He used to wait on twenty-four to thirty customers on a Saturday. He would sort of sweep them up when they wanted a bathing suit or a pair of underwear or a pair of socks. We taught him that it is better to take a few minutes and really profile each customer, which meant he would "wait on" fewer customers, but he would develop personal relationships with some of them. He's managed to do that, and his total sales have increased. He's also turned many customers into clients.

What happens is, associates end up literally running their own little businesses within our business. A perfect example is Rita Roman. She has a nucleus of 231 clients. She knows a lot about the husband and the wife (she usually has both as clients), as well as their kids, their cats, their jobs, and their travel plans. Believe me, when the computer goes down, or there is no paper in the printers, we instantly know it, because Rita is shouting that she hasn't gotten her reports to service her customers.

A lot of businesses heap extra attention on their top customers, but they make the mistake of just about totally ignoring the bottom, to the point of being rude to the smaller spenders. We will never forget the base of the pyramid. They are real individuals, wonderful people, and we must hug each and every one of them, every visit. After all, if you lose the bottom of the pyramid, your volume base is gone. Your sales have just dropped by 20 percent, and 80 percent of your customers are gone, and who wants that? Besides, you need to add to the top of the pyramid, and the best way to do that is from the bottom. A lot of people shop at several stores until they find the one they're most comfortable with. They might not spend that much at any one of those businesses until they find the one that really serves them, and then they'll go there for all of their needs. So a cardinal principle of ours is *Never, ever, forget the bottom.*

The minute our associates step on the selling floor, all women and men are created equal.

I was recently on a flight to London with some friends, sitting in the back of the bus in coach. I always travel coach, my choice unless I can find some way of getting upgraded, like frequent flier mileage. Most of the time the trips are fine—or acceptable. But this time, sitting at the bottom of the pyramid on the 777, I really felt like I was part of the 80 percent. I was treated not much better than a stowaway. I looked around, and I was surrounded by a lot of men and women also being treated like third-class cattle. There was very little engagement from the attendants. Only one of them really smiled and seemed to be having fun. The food was almost inedible. There was no legroom. At one point, I got whacked in the knee by the cart going up and down the aisle, and the attendant not only didn't apologize, she didn't even ask if I was OK. I might have been better off in baggage.

No one should be treated like that. We know that, year after year, smaller spending customers come in and they are very loyal, and we appreciate that. They should feel like they are flying business or first class, never coach. With our technology, as we track them and get to know them better and educate them about clothing, they too begin to spend more. Really almost every Saturday a customer will come up to me and say, "I'm not the biggest customer in the world, but that young man, Chris, took so much time and energy and effort with me to select the perfect tie for my husband for his high school reunion." These customers are moved to come and tell me because they are blown away by our service. I love that!

In fact, we've recently established a new category that we follow in the computer in a similar manner to clients, which is the "advocate." Here the benchmark or criteria aren't dollars. An advocate is someone who frequently shops with us and they constantly brag about our stores and recommend us or one of our associates to their friends and business colleagues. These are customers that may easily find themselves neglected at many stores, because their dollar volume may not put them up there with the big spenders, but their advocacy is an unrecognized bonus, which we find extremely important to the growth of our business. My dad always said, "Jack, you'll learn the best advertising is word of mouth."

Advocates are wonderful, because not only are they spending money in the store, but they also are bringing in additional customers. If someone at Merrill Lynch or Lehman Brothers says to an associate of theirs that Marilyn or Bob at Mitchells, or Arlyne or Amy at Richards, is better than sliced bread, or Arthur says to his neighbor that Mitchells has the best customer service in the world, these men and women have felt the hugging culture and are passing it on.

There's one other category of customer that exists throughout the pyramid: the "difficult customer." Let's face it, in any business some customers are awfully demanding. The guy who has the painter come back and paint the living room three times until the shade is just right. The guy who has to test-drive thirty cars until he finally picks the one he drove first. Far too many businesses tell these people to take their business elsewhere. In effect, they fire the customer.

I love demanding customers. Once you've won them over, they're customers forever. But there are customers that push us too far. In more than thirty years, I can only recall three customers that I fired.

They were rude and impossible to please. They would actually swear at associates, and the alterations, no matter how perfectly we did them, were never good enough. When this happens, there's only one alternative. Politely tell them to shop elsewhere.

But you should never be too hasty. We'll make a note in our system if someone is very demanding about certain things, and work extra hard at them. Time after time, we find that the "difficult" customers are testing us, and once we establish a good relationship with them, they often become the best customers of all.

Chapter 30

One on One

Our technology works hand in hand with something we're really known for, which is our marketing. Cool, hip, funny, WOW seem to be the words most often associated with great advertising. Yet most customers just want to know why they should buy something from you. What makes your company different is most important to them. Marketing must know the customer. Marketing must hug.

We call our style of marketing "relationship" or "one-on-one" marketing. It's highly personalized, and an important criterion of any marketing we do is that it must further the relationship.

Just as all politics is local, most buying decisions are local. Most people rely on a small group of trusted friends and business associates. If you can turn one person into a loyal fan, you'll get plenty of new customers.

We do all the conventional things like run newspaper and magazine ads. We also do things like give away good wooden hangers with our name on them to local beauty salons, day spas, and restaurants, because when customers of those places hang up their coats they see our name and maybe give us a try. We send out a seasonal "image piece," and drop it in the Westchester County and Connecticut sections of the Sunday *New York Times*. It's shot on location at places like Anguilla and Tuscany. And we publish *Forum* magazine, our own men's editorial magazine, which has articles on everything from recent trends in fashion by Bob Mitchell to heli-skiing to shopping for a private island.

We have found we don't need some expansive, hierarchical marketing department to handle all this. My son Andrew does all of it—with some outside assistance from freelance graphic designers. We're talking about coordinating dozens of events and tens of thousands of mailings a season with a staff of two—plus, of course, our adjunct staff of 194 associates. For the crucial thing we've realized is that the true marketing is accomplished by having great sales associates. They are really the marketing department. They get the customers in the store and coming back year after year.

Marketing must move from the bottom up, not the top down. Many times we say to our great sellers, We want to invest in you. We would rather pay you more than pay to put additional ads in the *Westport News* or the *New York Times*. Most retail stores traditionally spend 3 to 5 percent of their sales on marketing. Years ago, we did too. But then we realized that we could spend less and invest it in great people. It was a tremendous win for everyone.

One of our associates came to my office during the recession of 1990–91 saying we needed to do more advertising. And I said, "Better yet, you need to call some customers or write to them."

The thing we really pride ourselves on is the highly targeted marketing that technology allows us to do and that our associates execute. We don't do any mass mailings. It's all targeted to specific customers in a personalized way.

Not long ago, for example, we programmed the computer to produce a list of all customers who hadn't made purchases in more than two years and those that hadn't spent more than $900 for a suit. There were three thousand names on the list, and we sent out direct mail to all of them and invited them to visit the store for a special promotion. It worked out beautifully. Four hundred and thirty-eight of the three thousand customers, an excellent response for a mailing, came in and made a purchase. We generated $313,000 in sales.

We also do target mailings based on a customer's preferences in clothing manufacturers, notifying them when a favored maker's "trunk show" is going on in the store. (A trunk show is when a line of clothes is shipped to a store for a few days for customers to examine; it got the name when peddlers used to bring the merchandise around in trunks.) We've even begun sorting out in the computer sales by street address. We can isolate that we're selling a ton of clothing on a given street, and then we'll look at the addresses. We'll find out that nothing is being sold to 62 Vine Street, and so that family becomes a hot prospect to try to develop a relationship with.

Because we track every purchase a customer makes, we are able to customize our business with them. When our buyers go into the market, they purchase specifically for "Dan" or "Tom." At times, they literally tailor their buys for an individual customer, but they always visualize different "types" of customers, different profiles of customers. They see a new model, or silhouette, color, or fabric, and they say, "Who would buy this? Would Larry buy this, or would Paul?" They think this way and execute this way because they know the Larrys and can remember the Pauls, their tastes, their profiles, their businesses, their pleasures—because they touch the customer. They have been on the floor. They can go beyond the printout reports they have been working from.

Say a customer travels all the time. Ermenegildo Zegna has a suit called the Traveler that comes in a high-performance twist fabric that a man can wear in economy class and still step off the plane looking good enough to enter the boardroom. Or if he's a first-class guy, we might put him in a 15 Mil Mil, which is Zegna's top-of-the-line cloth that looks and feels like cashmere.

Recently, we introduced Giorgio Armani Black Label for Women at Richards, an exciting new collection for us. Linda thought she would need to buy two seasons' worth without yet seeing how the garments fit. (A size 8 in one designer line may be very different in another.) Here again, our technology helped her out big time. We received some clothes early, and our passionate sales associates broke open the boxes in the basement and brought them to the dressing rooms for their clients and sold them, even before we opened the new shop. That very night, just before Linda left for Milan to buy the second season, she ran a report that detailed these sales, plus she ran a list of our top fifty Richards women's customers and their sizes. Technology (with a little help from our enthusiastic hugging associates) gave her an extra edge when she sized the order in Armani specifically for our Greenwich customers.

When you combine technology with your associates' know-how, you achieve one-on-one marketing that furthers the relationship.

Chapter 31

We Like to Drop a Line

Marketing means keeping in touch with the customer, not just waiting to see them in the store. We're big on writing notes, lots of them, and technology helps us make sure they're always personal.

When I wake up in the morning, I get a printout on my home printer of every sale of at least $2,000 from the previous day. It's the report I love the most, so it comes out first. It shows the entire profile information on the customer and spouse, plus what sales associate sold what to them. I like to know those sales, because they're significant and I want to thank those involved in them. Usually I'll punch F6, which pulls up a screen that allows me to communicate to Pamela Miles, my fabulous assistant, to draft a note to the customer. I'll also make sure to congratulate the sales associate for a super-important sale.

Meanwhile, associates often send out personalized notes of their own. It could be a birthday card or an anniversary card or simply a note to say hi. When we send out a personal letter, it's really personal, because it has details we could only know by checking the computer. Even a computer-generated letter has a real, positive impact, especially if it is signed in ink with a handwritten personal note. That's what we aim for. Everything should be personalized. So we sift through the computer to give us the facts on a customer's recent visit to the store and use that as a springboard for a note that reads as if it were hand-crafted. One of the other benefits of technology is our tracking system that lets us monitor the letters that went out so we don't duplicate any or flood someone with letters.

We address most of the envelopes by hand or by a sophisticated envelope printer and put real stamps on them, no bulk postage. That way it is more intimate and won't get thrown out. The chances are, if it's addressed by hand and has a real stamp, the person will open it and say, "Wow, they remembered my birthday." Our sales associates handwrite the birthday cards.

The conventional wisdom is that people don't want any more mail—they already get too much—but we've found that if it's personalized and specific to the customer, they love it. Out of the hundreds of thousands of letters we've sent out, maybe two or three people have said, "Enough already."

Here is an example of one letter I sent out recently:

Dear Sonny,

Thank you so very much.

I am delighted to have seen that you were in Richards on Saturday and bought beautiful items from Richard Laidlaw. I espe-

cially hope you will enjoy your Hickey-Freeman tuxedo and Canali sport coat.

Thank you very much for these purchases and, more important, thank you for your loyalty.

We treasure our relationship with you.

Warmest personal regards,
Jack

Here's another—a first-time-customer letter:

Dear Judy,

Thank you very much for shopping with us on Thursday.

I sincerely trust you were very pleased with all aspects of your shopping experience—especially our selection of Robin Rotenier jewelry.

I hope Michele Romano exceeded your expectations in regard to her professional service. I know that Michele looks forward to working with you in the future.

Never hesitate to call me personally—nothing is more important to me than having you and your family feel extremely satisfied when you visit either of our stores—it's the Mitchells mission.

Warmest regards,
Jack

Notice how there are certain similarities, but, importantly, personal touches and bits of information that make each letter very individual.

The computer gives us the information, and we always refer specifically to the purchases, the associate, and the date. You can only do this with a computer system that captures this detail, and the beyond-expectation hug is signed by the CEO or president or general manager or sales associate with a real pen and a handwritten note that says, "Thank you!"

The latest way we stay in touch with our customers is through a new program called New Arrivals. In Westport, we have a room with a digital camera that we use to shoot pictures of clothes. The pictures are stored in the computer. Say the latest Missoni line comes in. We shoot pictures of the items, and then we run a search and come up with the top fifty Missoni customers at our stores. We send out the pictures and tell them here are the newest items, you might want to come in and try some on. We'll also photograph trunk shows and send the pictures to customers who weren't able to get into the store to see the shows.

And then we do something else. Say a woman comes in and admires a piece of jewelry. The sales associate tells the marketing side. We photograph it and send the picture to the husband. We tell him, "Your wife was in the store the other day and she just loved this bracelet. Christmas is coming up [or her birthday or their wedding anniversary], and you might consider it as a gift." The guy is thanking his lucky stars. He's been obsessing over what to get her for two weeks, and everything he usually gets her she ends up returning. Now he's got a sure-fire gift, and all he has to do is respond and we'll send him the gift, wrapped and all. He never has to leave his desk. He does his shopping in five seconds.

By neatly wedding technology with marketing, you please your customers and generate additional sales.

HUGGING STUDY GUIDE #4

Technology must support hugging—technology is the backbone of any great company, and it should be designed to help you understand your customers and their needs. Many times businesses must adapt because "that's the way the technology works." Spend a little more and get a system that works for you. It must be simple, everyone should have access to it, and everyone, including the CEO, should endorse the system and be able to use it.

Layer in customers first—most systems focus on inventory or financial issues and often ignore the client base; to sell effectively, your system should layer in the customers before the product so you know every item your customers buy and a lot about who those customers are. But that customer data is sacrosanct. Never share it and never sell it, or you've violated the basic trust of the customer relationship.

Use the data—most businesses gather data, but don't know how to use it. Use it to anticipate needs and track who's selling what.

Technology allows you to control your inventory—you don't want too much inventory or too little. Technology allows you to have just the right amount.

Climb the pyramid—you have to focus on the customers that buy the most, without ever forgetting the bottom.

One-on-one marketing—technology enables you to personalize your marketing efforts and accomplish true one-on-one, or relationship, marketing. That way all marketing furthers the relationship.

Drop a line—to further the relationship, use your technology to write personalized letters to your customers.

PART FIVE

Game Day

It's about Playing to Win

Chapter 32

Aim to Win

I often hear businesses talk about how they're "having a good year" or they're "doing fairly well" or "things are looking solid." In today's world, that sort of vague thinking doesn't cut it. To be truly successful in business and reach your hugging potential, you have to think in terms of playing to win.

A few years ago, when I was playing tennis early one morning with my son Bob, it came to me why I love the retail game. Every day, whether it's a small day or a big day, we win or we lose. We're above plan or below plan. In high school, I was proud to be elected captain of the basketball, football, and baseball teams, and even then I really liked motivating, leading the rah, rah, rah and getting the players enthused and playing the game up to our best potential. Before every game, no matter how formidable our competition, I always envisioned winning. Of course I knew we wouldn't always win. And I learned at a very early age how to lose with grace and dignity—they used to call it being a "good sport." But I always imagined winning. I love to win.

I always had in my mind this inner game of winning, and I was able to refine it when I read *The Inner Game of Tennis*, by Tim Gallwey. Tim outlines three types of life goals: **enjoyment** goals, **learning** goals, and **performance** goals. So what really clicked in my head that morning when I was playing with Bob was that I loved retail because all three inner goals were sort of interacting at once: 1) the enjoyment goals—I love coming to work and hugging customers; 2) the learning goals—going to the stores is like going to school, because I pick up new ideas to improve the business when I encounter both new and loyal customers; and 3) the performance goals—it's easy to measure the results of having fun and learning, because you keep track of the score, the sales recorded by your players and how they compare with your targets. You win some and you lose some.

If all three goals are interacting in a positive, synergistic way, you usually win the game, but even if you lose, you feel like a winner because you've had fun and enjoyed it, and you've learned and grown. And that helps you win next time out.

Hugging organizations are best able to reach their potential when they have this winning attitude. We've found that one of the best ways to acquire the attitude is by thinking of business as a game. I really feel that anyone who is a real professional and who truly excels, whether as an administrative assistant, a life insurance salesman, a river guide, a taxicab driver, or a magazine publisher, will benefit by following some of the disciplines of sports, by thinking of their work as a game, with fun and learning for everyone, but that comes with a score and, ultimately, a winner and loser.

I'm always struck by how the business world mimics the sports world in so many ways. The captain of a team, just like the chief executive, has to profile his players and know their strengths, weaknesses, and hot buttons. In both cases, you have performance reports and key plays. In football, for instance, you're concentrating on steadily moving the ball down the field, and that's what we do in business. You have the small play—seven yards, or a first down, like selling a suit and tie, or a dress and scarf—and the big play—a long pass to the end zone, which would be like three suits, a sport coat, ten shirts. And then there's the extra point—the purchase of several ties, a couple of pairs of shoes, and a matching belt, sort of as an afterthought.

When you think in terms of a sports analogy, you realize that every business has its pivotal games—the days or months or seasons that are critical in determining your year. You have to make an extra effort during those big games and the playoffs. Nearly half of our business is transacted on Saturdays, and so we refer to Saturday as Game Day. It's when we have to perform at our best and call our smartest plays. Then we consider the Saturdays in December as the playoffs. And we think of the Saturday before Christmas or Hanukkah, when people arrive in droves to make their last-minute gift purchases, as the Super Bowl.

Game Days are the ultimate test of the effectiveness of your hugging organization. I once heard this great definition of an entrepreneur: An entrepreneur says, "Give me the ball." He's the guy who wants to take the last shot when the big game is on the line. The best hugging organizations are made up of entrepreneurs, and every single one of them wants to take the last shot on Game Day. Because they have the *passion to win* the game.

Chapter 33

The Three P's = Profits

If you're going to win the big games, you have to **plan, prepare, and practice** for them before you begin to play, and that's what leads to **profits**. These are what I call the **Three P's**.

By "plan," I mean you need to have a certain foundation of basic knowledge stored in your head. By "prepare," I mean you need a systematic body of prepared material—some sort of playbook—at your disposal, from which to call your plays. And when I speak of "practice" I mean you don't try out plays for the first time during the big games.

This sequence happens on several levels, but for management, there are five sets of business information you need to memorize to **plan** for the daily game.

1. **All associates' names (first and last).** For your key associates, try learning their spouses' and children's names. Obviously you can't do this completely in a large company, but we think that at least 250 names is not a big deal. A lot of people say, "Oh, come on, that's far too many." Well, I point out that before the age of six more than a billion Chinese learn the 214 radicals (Chinese characters) they need to know in order to look up words in their dictionary. So the mind can do it, if you have the desire, the passion.

   I recently met Peter Grauer, the new chairman of the Bloomberg operation who took over when Michael became the mayor of New York. I was blown away by his top priority. It was so wonderful. He said he flew the world, meeting and greeting all eight thousand members of the Bloomberg empire. To me, that was eight thousand hugs. Now of course he didn't meet every single one, but that was his mindset—the people and the hugging—and when I got a tour of the Bloomberg building, I saw the openness of the offices, and my impression was he knew at least 214 associates as he went from department to department saying, "Hi Iwonya," "Hi Joe." When you know your associates' names, that makes them feel like family.

2. **The names of the top one hundred customers.** We believe the top two fifty, five hundred, or a real stretch of a thousand would be fabulous, but not to know your top hundred is just criminal. At many businesses, many senior executives don't even know the customer. The attitude is so often, "It's not my job or responsibility. I'm in the financial [or purchasing or

even the marketing] end. The salesmen are supposed to know who the customers are, not me." But the hugging culture must start at the top. The CEO's primary job is to make sure everyone is hugging and customers are happy. To know they're happy, he needs to know who they are.

3. **Top line sales for the day, month, and year.** You should also memorize the critical benchmark numbers for your current year and two years back, and know the projections for two years forward. Plus, you need to be able to put your hands on the details at a moment's notice. If you don't know the numbers, how can you tell how you're doing?

4. **Gross margins by percentage for the month,** the year to date, and again going back two years and going forward two years. Buyers should know these by categories, by departments, by heart.

5. **Pretax profit.** This, too, you need to know going back several years and going forward. Obviously if you know the percentage pretax and you know your margins, you can quickly get an estimate of your total expenses.

We're always amazed at how few business leaders rarely know all of these straightforward things. If you don't, you're starting the game a touchdown or two behind.

To **prepare** for our encounters on the selling floor, we have a book that we actually call the Play Book. Each sales associate gets his or her own individualized Play Book each week, on Monday morning. The purpose is to provide associates with all the data necessary to prepare for the week, particularly Game Day, and to facilitate communications from management.

The Play Book enables associates to look at these reports as part of the game and have fun with them (Goal No. 1), to learn more about their customers and clients and to figure out new ways to enhance their selling and hugging relationships (Goal No. 2), and to increase performance and sell more product in the long run (Goal No. 3).

The book is divided into two parts. The first part is a group of core reports that doesn't change from week to week. The second part includes lists that are time sensitive, like call lists for events.

These are the core reports:

> **Letters**—there will be at least a letter from the store manager and me. More often than not, I try to stress some sort of hugging story that occurred the previous week, or opportunities I see coming up in the current week. Several times, I have actually quoted from letters I received, or the store received from customers thanking us for extraordinary service. Obviously this is an opportunity for me to hug all our associates. In addition, these letters outline the priorities for the week and serve as a standard communications tool. They update any contests and announce important events.

> **Sales Associate Future Schedule**—this shows each associate's normal day off and any future days he or she won't be in the store. This helps management prepare; you need your best players on the field for the big games. Of course people are out, they go

on vacations (you have to rest and recharge your superstars), they get sick—so you need backups, or pinch hitters, to play the game.

➤ **Calendar**—this lists all upcoming events in the store. If "NEW" appears in front of the item, that means it has been added or changed in the last two weeks.

➤ **Sales Associate Report with Goals**—this gives the associate's completed sales for the week, month, and year to date.

➤ **Client Report**—this shows all clients as of the previous Saturday, and their activity. (Remember, for us, our internal working definition of a client is any customer who has spent more than $5,000 in any of the last three years.)

➤ **Potential Clients**—this lists all customers of the associate who aren't clients but have spent at least $3,500 in the last twelve months, close enough perhaps for the associate to elevate to a client with a bit more attention to other parts of his or her wardrobe. Maybe they have bought only business wear and have been buying their weekend wear at another store.

➤ **Promised Alterations**—this shows all alterations scheduled for the week. The idea is to use the pickups as an appointment. In a perfect world, it is scheduled and the associate is prepared at a minimum to be there when the customer tries on the garments. In many cases the associate can use the occasion as an opportunity to sell related items, like scarves and shoes, that complete the outfit.

➤ **Special Orders**—this shows the status of special orders, both those that have and have not been received, and those not sold or picked up.

➤ **Satisfaction Report**—this includes all items that came out of the tailor shop two or three weeks ago. Associates are expected to call all customers on the list to make sure they are extremely satisfied with their shopping experience and their alterations. It is especially important to call any customer who is a first-time shopper.

➤ **Client Profile with Next Steps**—this is vital, because it lists next steps to do for customers and clients, which are essential to cultivating relationships. For example, an associate might promise a customer that he will call him in the fall for the Zegna trunk show. Or a client's birthday or wedding anniversary is coming up, and the associate wants to send a card and flowers. So the associate enters these things into the system. Next steps start printing out two weeks before the due date and continue for four weeks after the due date.

We've obviously tailored the Play Book to our own specific needs, but you can see how, with minor variations, you can devise one for any type of business, whether it's financial services or health care or canned fruit. I've always felt airlines are sorely in need of a Play Book. Imagine if the captain prepared a Play Book for each flight so the flight attendants knew their customers' names, remembered their favorite beverages—coffee, tea, soda, or a martini extra dry—with a genuine smile and actually thanked them for their previous trip. Imagine if you were able to make your connecting flight with time to spare because, without even asking, they assigned you a seat close to the front. Imagine if your video store had a Play Book, and, knowing that you like action movies, called you up to tell you when *Die Hard 7* had arrived. Customers would eat this up.

Once you're done planning and preparing, you have to **practice**. And you have to be disciplined about it, not practicing only when you feel like it or you're bored. Great sellers will spend time at night, or in the morning before the store opens, reviewing their Play Book or looking in the mirror and rehearsing imaginary encounters with customers.

We actually hold practice games at the store, either before or after hours. The way they work is, we divide the associates into teams of five or six. Each team is handed an index card with a different customer description on it. One card might read: "Investment banker. 45 years old. Has to travel a lot. Likes double-breasted and pin-striped. Looking to buy two new suits and a golf outfit for an outing. 43 Regular."

Once they've digested their assignment, each team has exactly seven minutes to race around and pick appropriate outfits. We clock them with a stopwatch. Then each team chooses one member to "sell" the selections in front of everyone else. Once all the teams have finished their presentations, everyone votes on who did the best job of selecting and selling the clothes. The members of the winning team receive $20 apiece.

We especially like to run these practice games when a new season is beginning and the store is full of fresh merchandise, because these exercises help acquaint the sellers with the new product.

This **plan, prepare, practice** sequence is the surest way to **profits.** I always like to tie the word "profits" to the other p's so the players know they're playing for the bottom line.

Chapter 34

Everyone on the Field

On Game Day itself, everyone's primary focus has to be the floor. Their total mindset must be helping the customers and assisting sales associates with their every need.

There's no way you can win without the whole team. In football, the guards and tackles are extremely important in opening the holes for the running backs. In our business the guards and tackles are the buyers and the credit managers and the tailors, without whom the running backs would not score the touchdowns. In bad economic times, you obviously need the defense as well, which focuses on inventory control and is prudent with every expense, but then you quickly send in the offense when you see a chance to make a field goal. You can't win unless you score.

And it's very important that nobody sits on the bench. All the players must have the thrill of playing the game with passion. If they don't, you need to trade or send them to another team.

And so we believe that everyone, not just the sellers, but the controller, the credit manager, and the buying assistants should focus only on customers on Game Day, and not on their "other jobs," no matter how much work they have piled on their desk. (Believe me, these other jobs are critical to the success of our business, so it's very important that they understand how vital being on the floor on Game Day is to the hugging culture of the business.) Sure, there may be dead time, because customers come in like waves. For body surfers, it's that sixth wave, and we're always braced for that one too.

If it's your biggest day, the owner has to be there. It's like that old expression: "You have to fish where the fish are." Next time you buy something on a weekend or holiday, ask for the owner. If the service is awful, the odds are the owner is out actually fishing, or putting out on the ninth hole.

We always start big selling days with a meeting to get everyone enthused. It's the same as a locker-room pep talk or, in a sense, a huddle. I always loved the camaraderie of the huddle. Everyone is thinking of the team. You have your own latitude, but you're also dependent on others. You could make a terrific sale, but if the tailor shop or the shipping department drops the ball, you're not getting any yardage. You may even be penalized ten to fifteen yards for the error.

What everyone learns is that some people may be *independent* personalities and others may be *dependent* types, but when you explain that on a team everyone is *interdependent,* all the members feel good. On our team, there is a relationship where everyone depends on one another— a true interdependent environment. And that interdependence leads to *synergy*, where $1 + 1 = 3$. Or sometimes 4 or 5, or maybe even 11!

I know it sounds corny, but it works: the mindset of all the players must be team, team, team, profile, profile, profile, hug, hug, hug.

Chapter 35

Do Your Own Lights

The look of the playing field itself makes a big difference in how you perform. I'm referring to big things—is the carpet worn, are the walls smudged?—and little things. I was at the doctor's the other day and all the magazines in the waiting room were months out of date. Who wants to read issues of *Time* and *Newsweek* previewing the congressional elections three months after Election Day? It made me wonder if the doctor liked to read ancient history or if he was just cheap.

In our case, the playing field means store design, visuals, and display. We've often had a problem with store designers, because it's clear to us that their No. 1 priority is design and image, not customers. Customers want convenience and product. Designers want "interesting," "wow," "pretty," "mood." Take lighting, a very important part of a store. Often designers want mood. Customers like to see the product.

When we built the new Richards store, we used top-notch architects and designers, but if we found they weren't thinking of the customer's needs, our culture of a friendly hugging environment, we went our way. We fired one of the world's "premier lighting consultants," whom our architects brought to us because they wanted mood lighting. People might like mood lighting when they're sitting down to a romantic dinner, but when they're shopping they want lights that allow them to see the clothing. Is the dress blue or black? My son Russ, who oversaw the construction of the store, insisted on two thousand light fixtures recessed into the fourteen-foot ceilings.

Convenience is extremely important to customers. You have to arrange the field so that it's not a secret where the fitting rooms and return desk are. Everything from parking to checkout needs to be easy. I'm sure you've been in a store and were going to buy something and you looked up and you saw this god-awful line and you said, "Aw, the heck with it." We monitor these things constantly, and when lines form, we recruit all available hands, including the presidents of the business, to run the registers.

No matter how well you design things, though, new customers who aren't familiar with your business require a little extra assistance, because they feel tentative in a new territory. They need to get space, get the feel of the land, so we tell them to make themselves at home. We might say, "Here's where the clothing is," "Here's where the sportswear is," and it's often useful to walk them around.

How many places have you been where they say, "It's over there," rather than walking you to the area you asked about. It's a little detail, a little hug, but this is especially true with the ladies' room or the men's room. Many times I judge a restaurant's potential by how they show me where the men's room is. Do they say it's downstairs or upstairs, or do they literally walk me toward it until it's perfectly clear where it is? Usually the quality of service at dinner reflects this tiny detail.

Chapter 36

Be a Mirror

No business can win its game without great product. In any business, you have to make a choice between whether you're going to give your customers what you think they ought to buy or what they tell you they want.

In our case, we've always tried to be a mirror of the community. In the early days, for instance, we used to sell nothing but Arrow and Hathaway shirts, because that's what was right for our clientele. Our customers didn't even know it was possible to have a shirt custom-made. Our community changed. Now a third of the shirts we sell are made to measure.

When casual Friday spread through the business world, executives weren't sure what to do. We adjusted our own inventory and helped them understand the casual revolution at work—sport coats and turtlenecks and, yes, even khakis.

We listen instead of preach.

One thing we hear is that many customers want help in how to use our product. There's been all this talk about how they're making manuals for electronic equipment and appliances easier than ever to read, but they still read like Sanskrit to me. And then when I ask an appliance salesman to explain the controls on a dishwasher, he talks in Sanskrit.

Helping the customer know how to use your product has never been more important, because product choice and sophistication is greater than ever. That's certainly true in our business. Dress has changed a lot from the days when in the business world you had to wear a suit everywhere. We're in what's been called the appropriate dress environment. A top executive, like Nick Donofrio of IBM, can stroll through the technology section of his company wearing a sport coat and a casual knit shirt, and that's fine. But then the same day he has to attend a board meeting of the Bank of New York, where everyone is wearing a suit, or fly to a business meeting breakfast the next morning in Arizona, where the appropriate dress calls for casual wear. Indeed, Nick's assistant told us that she calls ahead and asks what the expected dress is to give Nick a heads up on what he should wear for his diverse appointments.

I've coined a name for today's challenge: the "Clark Kent syndrome." Just as Clark Kent had to keep a change of clothing ready so he could switch on a moment's notice, so too does the modern businessman or woman have to keep alternatives always on hand.

To help Clark Kent dress, we print a booklet for men on how to dress appropriately, with a lot of detail on what to wear when, and how to put outfits together. If you are the leader of a hugging company, it seems obvious to me it's the sort of thing you ought to do for your customers, whatever your specialty. We invite our customers to come to one of our seminars, "The Business of Dress." And if they'd like help putting their wardrobe together, we can do that too. It's a free wardrobe consultation. That goes for women as well as men. And nobody will push you to buy. Our clients tell us they love and enjoy these hugs.

So don't just sell product. Help your customers understand how to use it. Then they'll come back not only for your product but also for your advice.

Chapter 37

Visit the Territory

One of the important ways you make sure you get great product when you need it, and therefore get an edge in the game, is by hugging your vendors or suppliers. (And don't forget to hug your bankers, too, so you're able to finance your purchases.) One of the books that has had the greatest impact on me is *African Genesis* by Robert Ardrey. It demonstrates that humans evolved from animals in Africa and shows how we inherited an instinct for territoriality that dominates our relationships. It discusses the power of "Number One," the herd, and the "we-they" instinct.

Most important, it makes clear his point that our relationships all revolve around territory. I had always thought that our relationships are about sex and hunger. They're important, but Ardrey emphasizes the most powerful instinct of man: the animal instinct of territoriality. Which is not to forget that we have this wonderful thing called a brain that can override these instincts.

At Mitchells/Richards, we make a point of going to people's offices or factories—to their territory. It's a huge hug for our vendors when we go to their home base. I learned this very quickly when I went the first time to Rochester, New York, to visit Hickey-Freeman. Who wants to go to Rochester? We do!

You can get most everything done in New York, Milan, or Paris? Wrong!

Who wants to go to Baltimore, as we used to with our buyers in the old days, or to Bangor, Maine? We do.

Because what happens is, we meet someone in the shipping department of Hickey-Freeman or Cole-Haan and by remembering their name and writing a note saying thank-you for shipping these hundreds or thousands of jackets or shoes over the years, they remember us. They really appreciate it, and you can bet they'll be there to help us out when we need an emergency shipment. It's not as sexy as going to Europe, which we also do—and in fact we were told we were among the first American retailers years ago to actually go through the Armani factories in Turino, Italy—but it's effective. So see the people on their turf. They'll love the gesture. And you listen and you learn, and you build a relationship that is a lasting one.

And you'll find they'll hug you back. When Umberto Angeloni, CEO of Brioni, invited Bill and me to go on safari in South Africa, that's a hug back. And in the bush we learned more about Brioni and their dreams and strategies, and we shared ours with him.

Our relationship with Zegna truly epitomizes how two families have reached out to each other from every department and part of their businesses. At the top, Gildo Zegna and I have developed a personal relationship, as has my son Bob, who is more Gildo's generation. Plus, Bob and I have a relationship with his cousin and co-president Paolo and the other members of that Zegna generation. It goes on and on, with their buyers, designers, marketing, and computer systems executives. Richard Cohen, the president and CEO who, along with Bob Green, runs the North America operations, and our family constantly interact: We play golf together, we enjoy pasta together, we drink wine together, we send notes and cards to each other, and we hug—literally bear hugs—both in Connecticut and Italy.

Don't just call or e-mail your vendors. Get on a plane, bus, car, boat, or train and go see them.

Chapter 38

Ten Great Plays Will Win

Once you've prepared, got your field set, and acquired the best product, you're ready to call your plays. Our Play Book is pretty detailed, but to be successful you need maybe ten to twenty great plays, tops. You don't need a thousand. If you have too few, they get stale. If you have too many, even the best players can't learn them well enough to execute them properly. I don't want our associates writing plays on their arms the way football players do, and then if they get tackled and the ink smudges they go deep when they were supposed to catch a screen pass.

Here's one of the great plays in the Play Book. The sales associates have a page where they write in appointments with customers or clients who will, hopefully, be coming in on Saturday for new merchandise or to pick up previously purchased items. These sheets then go to someone who adds a "snapshot view" of their profile, and this sheet gets stapled to the cover sheet, so Bill and I are prepared to pile on the hugs when the customer or client comes in. Almost everyone loves to meet the leader, or a member of our family, who owns the business.

Another big benefit is that the sales associate gets to see the previous sales, and might notice that Jim hasn't bought a topcoat, or needs a new raincoat, or his wife, Arlene, has never shopped with us, and that when the appointment was made, Jim mentioned he might bring his wife. All this information, properly used by the associates, can turn a good sale into a great sale. That's what wins on Game Day.

When the customer comes in, an important play is to always try to do a little something different. It could be a cup of decaf cappuccino. It could be walking out to the car with their merchandise. If the customer is a soccer fan, it could be, "Isn't it great that the USA women won in soccer?" It's building the relationship.

There's a furniture store in Massachusetts where, when you drive around to the loading dock to pick up your chair or end table, one of the attendants washes the windows and tires of your car, and offers you a free hot dog. I love it.

Being ready for the little emergencies that crop up is a play we believe in that I rarely see elsewhere. On Game Day, everyone is run ragged, but in doing our scheduling for our tailor shop we always plan for around a dozen "specials," meaning unexpected jobs. So if someone comes in and a button comes off their jacket or dress, we sew it on while they're shopping. And a button always does come off.

One day, a customer was seated in the back of a car literally on his way to his wedding. He was understandably a little nervous, and he spilled coffee all over his pants. "Wait," he told the driver. "You've got to make a detour and stop at Richards. They're my only hope." He rushed in the door, and exclaimed, "I'm on my way to my wedding, and look at what I did to my pants." He didn't have to say another word. We mobilized the offense, got him a new pair of matching pants, altered them, and sent him on to his wedding with time to spare. It's no wonder that one customer, who ran the emergency room at Greenwich Hospital, used to say we run the clothes emergency room for Greenwich.

Not long ago, I had a problem with the window of my car, and I called the dealer to report it and said I was really busy, I didn't know when I could come in. The manager said, "How about if we send the mechanic over to you?" He came over and fixed the window in the parking lot. After that, do you think I'd ever go to another dealer?

We like to throw events. We're known for them. And these events are one of our crucial Game Day plays. We like to say there is always something happening at Mitchells and Richards, and there usually is. Events create an air of excitement, and who couldn't use a little more excitement in their lives? We hold trunk shows almost every Saturday, sometimes with models circulating through the store, and you can feel the extra charge of electricity in the air. People come to the store expecting these events.

Any regular events that people enjoy and anticipate are great plays. There's an orthodontist in Wisconsin who holds monthly contests— "Guess the staff's baby picture contest," "Count the yellow M&M's contest." The winner gets things like a family trip to Chuck E. Cheese's. I read about a laundromat in Virginia that stages a weekly "open mike" competition. They serve refreshments. People plan their weeks around it, and they draw a big crowd. While customers sing and tell jokes, their clothes are spinning in the washers.

Another great play: At most businesses, if a customer asks for something they don't carry, that's the end of the discussion. When that happens to us, we'll try to special order it or even buy it from a competitor at no profit for us. If it's a particularly difficult request, it really gets our interest.

I recall that years ago, we got a call from a client, who said, "Do you have any cowboy hats?" Well, it was a rare day that anyone who shopped with us needed a cowboy hat, so I said, "No, we don't, but we're in the clothing business, how can we help?" And he said, "I'm throwing a party for my brother and I'm going to have a Western theme. There'll be pony rides for the kids, and lassoes and everything. So I was figuring, what if I sent out cowboy hats with the invitations, and then the guests would show up wearing the hats?"

I said, "That sounds like a great idea. How many hats do you need?" "About a hundred and fifty," he said. You learn in business to always ask a customer how much he wants to spend, because you can never be sure, and people don't like surprises. So I asked him, and he said, "Oh about ten or fifteen dollars a hat." I said, "We'll see what we can do."

Well, I called up a hat manufacturer nearby. They said they didn't make cowboy hats, but they gave me the number of Stetson in New York. I called there and got the president. I explained my mission, and he laughed. "Ten or fifteen dollars a hat, are you kidding?" he said. Stetsons sold for about two or three hundred dollars. But one of the assistants on a return call told me about a place on the Bowery that made cowboy hats that they sold to the Far East. She said, "In Taiwan, everyone wants to be an American cowboy." I called the place up and explained to the owner what I had in mind. He said, sure, he had a hundred and fifty cowboy hats, and lots more. "How much do you want per hat?" I asked. He said right back, "How about four dollars each?" I thought, four dollars, they had to be awful. I sent someone down to pick up five hats. When he brought them back, I looked at them and they were terrific. So I sent him back to get the rest, we packed them up, and the customer was thrilled—all in the same day. Nice sale for the day, plus an extremely satisfied customer.

Six months later, I happened to be at a meeting in Lubbock, Texas, where they sell plenty of Stetsons. I always remember sizes, and I recalled that the client wore a size 7½. I bought him a beautiful Stetson, and when he came in to do his Christmas shopping—and he was in a great mood, picking up lots of presents for his friends and family—I gave it to him as a present. He went to heaven. The Stetson was a big hug. It was an appropriate expense that was not frivolous, because it was for a great customer, the expectations of whom we had long been exceeding.

That was quite a while ago, and we haven't had an order for a cowboy hat since, but when we do, we're ready.

Some plays don't result in a sale, but they foster goodwill. We have a customer who is one of the all-time shop-to-drop clothes horses. Gary comes in almost every Saturday, and often three or four other days a week, to schmooze and to buy. He's a very successful divorce attorney, and his wife always kids that if they ever get divorced, all she wants is her husband's closet. His wife, looking for a creative gift for him for Hanukkah, asked if we would allow him to work as a sales associate one Saturday. Of course we would.

He was so excited, he showed up at 7:30 in the morning, dressed in his best suit. We gave him a little orientation, but he didn't really need any. He had called a multitude of his friends and clients—he had profiled them perfectly, and was ready to hug—and they came in. He loved it. He put in a good, hard day and managed to sell, or at least help to sell, $9,778 worth of merchandise. We made a donation to his favorite charity as a hug to him for this fun day with us. He had such a terrific time, he wants to do it again.

Execute plays like these on Game Day and watch the points add up.

Chapter 39

Consistency Counts

This happens to me all the time. An acquaintance will recommend a great restaurant or a great hotel, but when I go there the food is in-edible or the front desk clerks treat you like you're an assassin. When I report my experience to the person who told me about the place, he'll say, "Oh, you must have caught them on a bad day."

Well, maybe I did. But that was the only day I was there. It doesn't do me any good if the day before and the day after, everything *was* great.

Winning teams perform at their best day in and day out. They're consistent. Consistency is delivery of what has come to be expected experience. It means delivering exceptional customer service the first time you encounter a customer, then doing it again the second time and the third time and the fortieth time.

Consistency is very important in any business. It is what trust is based on. It's why McDonald's is so fussy that its French fries are made identically at every franchise, every day. And if you deliver the same high level of service on your busiest days as you do on your quietest days, it really impresses customers. That has to be your goal.

Every associate must be consistent with every customer. Once you've found the hug that is appropriate for a particular customer, you need to use the same method of hugging in a *consistent* manner, which becomes the standard. It is important to remember the previous hugs. When I meet certain customers, I give them a bear hug. If I didn't, they would say to themselves, "Something is wrong." If I didn't walk out to the car with certain other customers, it just wouldn't feel right to them, or to me.

There's no question that consistency is one of the most difficult things to control. That's why you have technology systems. That's why you plan, prepare, and practice. But it takes more than these things.

You have to check, check, and double-check. I make a point of trying to do one sale myself every Saturday. It could be some underwear, it doesn't matter. But it keeps me attuned to what's going on so I can check that we're being consistent. If someone says to me, "Well, I want to get some over-the-calf black socks, and I want a dozen of them," and I can't find the dozen, then I know we're inconsistent with our inventory of over-the-calf black socks. Men buy socks like that a half dozen at a time in case the laundry eats them up or the kids steal them. Or somebody says, "Why don't you have purple socks? I've got these purple pants they'd go perfectly with." I'll look into it: Is there enough demand to carry a few purple socks? If there is, we'll start consistently carrying them. After I finish with the socks, I'll try to build the sale: Do you need some underwear, how about a tie, maybe a suit? Or if it's his wife's birthday, I'll introduce him to someone in our women's department.

Consistency means that if you're going to do anything for the customer, you have to do it for everyone, including someone you've never seen before. That means that a customer is more important than a mannequin. One Saturday years ago, Mitchells was really mobbed, and this couple came in who had never been there before. The wife asked if we had a certain tie in a green coloration. I flipped through the tie racks and couldn't find it. The woman nodded at a mannequin and said, "There it is." So I got up and removed it and took it downstairs to be steamed. Meanwhile, the couple browsed around and wound up buying several suits, a couple of sport jackets, and twenty-three custom shirts. As they were checking out, the woman said, "We were in a store in Stamford before we came here, and there was a tie on the mannequin that I liked and I asked the manager if he could take it off, and he said, 'Absolutely not, the visual department is coming out from New York today and the visuals have to be perfect.' "

Well, we like our visuals to be perfect too, but we like to please our customers even more, and our visual associates love it when a seller sells ties, scarves, or an entire outfit from a display. That's the idea of a display! Some businesses will disrobe a mannequin for their best customers, and even throw in the mannequin if they ask for it, but they'll insult an unfamiliar customer.

You have to be consistent with all of your customers. Inconsistent businesses have inconsistent profits.

Chapter 40

Get a Driver's License and a Suit

Businesses often forget this, but you can't simply exist in the community, you have to give something back to it. We believe in being responsible citizens. After all, the community is where the playing field is. That's where most of our customers live. People choose to live there because they like it and it reflects how they feel about life and the things they care about. If you reflect those same values, through caring for the town, customers think of you as "one of them." I'm always surprised how many local businesses don't lift a finger for the community and then wonder why they don't win more games.

There are the obvious things to do—like host charity fund-raisers, as we do. We always send out personal invitations to these events, *personally* signed with a real ink pen, sometimes with a little gift (a flower or a cookie), plus most of the time we follow up with a phone call.

And then there are the less obvious things. And it's these less obvious things that often make a key difference in helping you win the game.

When Lowell Weicker, a Richards advocate, became governor of Connecticut, one of my closest friends, Emil Frankel, became Commissioner of Transportation. Meanwhile, Lou Goldberg became Commissioner of Motor Vehicles. One day, Lou was downstairs at Mitchells getting a suit fitted, and he had his dander up. He was grousing about how he was trying to improve customer service at Motor Vehicles and yet save money. He wanted to open local Motor Vehicle offices spaced around the state, so if you needed to renew your driver's license you could do it nearby rather than have to drive to one of the few central offices. It would vastly improve customer service. But when he went to talk to the people at the Westport town hall, they blew him off and refused to give him any free space.

Emil happened to walk in and caught the tail end of Lou's rage. He said to Lou, "Listen, I've got all these old buses sitting around at Transportation. Why don't you take them and drive them from place to place and use them as mobile offices?" Lou perked right up. Then Bill, who had entered the discussion, volunteered a suggestion: "And you can park one of the buses in our parking lot. We've got plenty of room, as long as it's not on a really busy day."

And that's exactly what happened. Once or twice a month, a Motor Vehicle bus pulls into our parking lot and people line up to get their licenses renewed. But that's not the end of the story. Anytime Bill spies a line of people, he gets antsy and his eyes enlarge about five times. So when that bus arrives, Bill often trots out with a fistful of $10-off certificates and hands them out. He also offers everyone a free cup of coffee, and buys the driver a corned beef sandwich. And, I'll tell you, it's fun and it's friendly, and we've picked up a nice amount of business. So it's a hug to the community that also does the store some good—another one of those win-win situations.

Who would have thought you could sell suits by working with the Department of Motor Vehicles?

Chapter 41

It's Two O'Clock, What's the Score?

Scott Mitchell, my nephew and head of the women's business in Greenwich, said to his team the other day, "Ladies, if you don't know the score, how are you going to know whether or not you will win or lose the game?"

Most of them were only concentrating on having fun and learning about their clients, which of course is great, but Scott explained, "In addition, you need to know the score of the game if you're trying to achieve your performance goals." And what Scott meant was not just sales for the day, but things like average sale and number of customers.

Most stores don't have the technology to track these statistics, and can't tell their associates how many singles, doubles, triples, and home runs they have had. Because of our technology, at any time of the day, we know how we stand by the hour—how many customers have been in the store and how much they have bought compared to the same day last year. And, as the day unfolds, we actually take action to try to affect the numbers. After all, that's the point of knowing the score— to do something about it if you're on the losing end.

In both of our stores, sales associates and managers constantly check throughout the day to see how we're doing, probably no one more than me. I love looking at the score. When I see that we're way ahead of the comparable day last year, I feel just terrific. I think to myself what my mom, God rest her soul, used to say: "We can have another bag of peanuts."

We find that everyone loves to know the score. People want instant gratification. They like to see how they're doing. When they check the stats, the associates will say to themselves, "Two hours to go and we need a few thousand dollars more to beat last year. What are we going to do?" They dig in and focus even harder to listen to where there might be a surprise shot that will win the point, like suggesting a new line that is still in the basement and not even on the floor. Belinda actually did that recently, going down the three levels to the shipping and receiving area to bring up clothing for select customers. She was almost crying, because she wears stiletto heels and her feet were practically bleeding. But she hugged her clients and made some great sales.

One of the most effective things they do to work up that score is get on the phone and call customers and get them to come in. We often find that a lot of new associates, even some with years of experience under their belt, are timid or afraid of rejection. We put a big emphasis on phone skills, because the phone is an invaluable hugging tool. Our best sales associates are masters of the phone.

We like to tell associates, it's OK to call customers if you get permission. What does that mean? When you see a customer in the store and you want to follow up, you simply say, "Is it OK that I call you? Is there a good time to call?" If they say, "Sure, sometime after eight," you've got permission. Then you're not invading their privacy. You're not one of those annoying marketers that call to sell phone service when the customer is sitting down to his flounder.

Linda, my wife, hates to be called. To her, it's a total invasion of her privacy. One night the phone rang at dinner and I didn't recognize who it was and was ready to hang up when the guy yelled, "Wait a minute, I'm the painter, and your wife is expecting me to call at eight." Linda grabbed the phone from me. She had given permission, so she was eager to get the call. That's what it's all about.

Joe, one of our top associates, told me this little story: "I recently called a customer at work who has a small ad agency and invited him to come in to look at a special fabric from the new fall clothing. He told me the market is down, business is tough; he just doesn't have that jingle in his pocket. I assured him that he could come in whenever he feels up to it. But sure enough, the next Saturday, the gentleman showed up, explaining that since I was so nice to call, to ask about his family, his golf game, whatever, that he just wanted to stop in. And he bought a very expensive sport coat, and he loved it."

As the selling day winds down, we're on the floor and get a feel for whether we had a good day or not, and of course we check the scoreboard to see if our intuition matches our reality. And for sure the next morning I always turn to the computer in my home to get the precise results. How did we do? Did we win (did we exceed our plan)? Or did we lose (under plan)? Are we winning for the month, or losing for the month? By store, by department, by classification? And then I quickly move to who sold what. Who were the high scorers? And then I sort of update in my mind the batting averages and other vital statistics, like number of customers for each sales associate, and the average sale for the day, month, and year to date.

No matter what the final numbers say, you should never mope about a losing day. Most important, I reflect on what we have to do to have more fun, to learn more to produce the winning numbers next time out. Whenever I play tennis with someone and get beaten, as happens with younger players in particular, I always say to the person, "How can I improve my game? What one or two things do you see that I can work on to be better? Is it my drop shot, or my volley, or something else?"

After a tough day at the store, we ask ourselves, or our customers, what we could have done better, and we work on that for the next Game Day, and the one after that. You can bet we're looking to win those games. It's just a lot more fun to win.

HUGGING STUDY GUIDE #5

Think of selling as a game with a winner and a loser—and everyone must think of your big selling days (in our case, Saturdays) as Game Days that require heightened preparation and focus.

The Three P's—to win, you must plan, prepare, and practice before you play the game, and that's what leads to profits. This includes giving your associates a Play Book with the latest information on their customers that they can use to execute winning plays.

Everyone on the field—on Game Day, everyone forgoes their normal workload and focuses on the customer and selling.

Pay attention to your playing field—that's where the game is played, so make sure it looks good and is convenient for the customer.

Be a mirror—reflect the needs of your community in what products and services you offer; listen, don't preach.

Visit the territory—if you want to have the best product, go see your vendors or suppliers on their turf.

Execute a small number of great plays well to win—two won't do it, and a hundred is too many to learn, but a small nucleus of ten to twenty plays will allow you to win.

Consistency counts—it's what trust is based on.

Be involved; be committed to your community—after all, that's where most of your customers live.

Know the score—it's hard to win if you don't know the score, so it's essential to constantly track and measure your sales and the numbers behind the sales. Make it possible for everyone to have access to the system for the latest scores.

PART SIX

The Formula

Have an Economic Model

Chapter 42

Why Hugging
Makes You Money

I'll never forget my first business. I was probably eight or nine, and my family was living in the Compo Beach section of Westport. Like a lot of kids, I wanted to have some sort of "stand." Wherever I looked, I was surrounded by lemonade stands all crowded close to the entry of the beach, so I figured that lemonade was oversaturated. I decided I would go into the popsicle business. A niche in the market, something different.

With some needed help from my mother, I bought the ingredients, made the popsicles, packed them into a cooler, and went out searching for a location. I found a great one on the corner of my road, Roosevelt Road, and South Compo Road, just where the cars had to slow down after making a gigantic turn. Besides, I knew the parents of my friends would buy my first ones. I waved to them as they walked down toward the beach. I guess I had a little hugging in me even then, as I smiled and said, "How about a popsicle, homemade?" Of course they bought some, and so did their friends and a few others. Wow! I felt so great when I walked home that first day with $26.43 in my pocket.

I thought I was a millionaire.

Then Mom handed me a bill for $35.63 for the ingredients. I was stunned. In a flash I had learned the difference between profit and cash flow and the importance and the value of inventory.

When Dad and Mom started the clothing business, they were a lot more financially sophisticated than I was in the popsicle days, but there was a similar spirit about them. They built relationships with customers because that was their nature, not because they felt that was the best way to make a buck. They were just naturally warm people. Just like me with my popsicle stand, they were never overly focused on how much money the store made. They simply wanted to have fun and to stay in business and to care for customers. Over time, though, it became obvious that hugging customers had enormous financial benefits.

And a good thing, too. Because it does you no good if you hug your customers but don't make any money. Pretty soon, you won't be hugging anyone but your creditors, because you won't have a business.

Some private businesses act as if they're embarrassed to admit that they are profitable. Not me. I don't go jumping up and down and telling the world what our numbers are. We cherish the privacy that comes with our independence, but I have found, from time to time, that it's important to share with our associates and our suppliers that we are financially sound and fiscally conservative. It may seem obvious, but the fundamental reason it is so important to be profitable is that without profit the business has no long-term future. Indeed, I am proud to say we're profitable. After all, it's the American way.

So it's worth reviewing here the distinct financial advantages you will enjoy if you have a hugging culture.

➤ **You attract the best sellers,** who are more productive, since they make more but cost less as a percentage of sales. As I've said, it's more fun and more rewarding to work in a hugging culture, and so even sellers who are superstars elsewhere find they make more with us. They do better and we do better.

➤ **Traditional marketing costs are lower.** Marketing costs are lower in a hugging culture because your huggers are your marketers. Instead of having to run lots of expensive ads in the media that you are not sure your customers see, you build systems and processes that help your huggers market. You still need to do some general media, traditional advertising to help build your brand, but in terms of driving revenue, nothing works like your huggers. Instead of spending lots of money on advertising, we invest in technology that helps our associates to know their customers. We invest in smiles and thank yous. Smiles don't cost anything. Thank yous don't cost anything. There's a restaurant where they put a ten-minute hourglass on your table when you sit down. If someone doesn't take your order in ten minutes, you get a free meal. Word of mouth spread fast about that little gimmick, and people go to that restaurant because they know they will be waited on efficiently. And since the restaurant's skilled staff is superb at doing its job and invariably takes orders before the sand runs out, it costs the restaurant nothing.

➤ **Gross margins are higher,** because we sell more product at regular price. When you've developed a genuine relationship with a customer, where they trust you and know you'll be fair to them, they'll also be fair to you. That means they'll be less interested only in what's on sale or what's cheapest. Price won't be the paramount issue with them. And what does "regular price" mean anyway? If a woman buys a $500 dress at some department stores, she'll usually pay about $50 for alterations. She'll pay nothing at our stores, get the alterations the same day if she needs them, and enjoy a cup of coffee and a bagel. Plus she'll receive the "value" of a polite, professional sales associate who really knows her. So our $500 dress has enormous value added. At the same time, we never, ever want to be a dollar higher than any regular-priced store, and if we discover we are, we immediately bring the price into line. And we do go on sale at the end of the season. You know, I've always said, "A poor man needs a bargain, a rich man loves one."

➤ **The revenue stream is long term and not highly variable.** Since we don't focus on the next hot product but stay close to what our customers desire, we don't have the steep ups and downs and big markdowns that businesses that are too forward do. The relationships you build up with the customers mean that when they're ready to buy, they buy with us rather than shop around at five or six different stores. Our surveys show that our clients spend 65 to 70 percent of their clothing budget with us. During the recession of 1989–91, when our sales dipped like everyone else's, we did a "Suit Survey," in which we found that customers who hadn't bought a suit in two years from us hadn't bought one from anyone else either. They were cutting back until the recession ended, not going elsewhere. They remained our customers and started buying normally when the economy improved. Also, because we have these longtime relationships, our returns run much lower than they do at other businesses. If you think about it, it makes sense. When you profile your customers, obviously you get the right product and the right sizes. Therefore you get extremely satisfied customers, fewer returns, less squabble, only one trip to the store. Everybody wins!

➤ **Real estate costs are lower,** because we don't have to pay for the ultra-best location. As I mentioned earlier, Mom and Dad didn't start with the best location, and it's still that way. Neither Mitchells nor Richards is in the very best spot in town, because that's not essential when you've got loyal customer relationships built on a hugging culture. Our existing customers will tell their friends where we are, and they'll find us and our convenient large parking lots and become our new customers. We are what our industry calls a destination store. We don't have to depend on tons of new customers tripping across our store accidentally. When they find us, they're glad they did. And we can pass along services and savings to them.

Each of these five expense items can add a point or two to the bottom line. Total them up and you have a nice profitable business in an industry that is typically not very profitable. Total them up in any industry and you'll have more profit than most of your peers.

Chapter 43

The Formula Is Born

Hugging comes with mighty financial advantages, but you can lose them fast if you don't have a plan, a roadmap that everyone follows when it comes to spending money.

Here's a simple question that many businesses get wrong. What is the biggest asset your company has?

A favorite answer in my industry is "inventory." Or some will say "real estate." Or what about cash in the bank? Or accounts receivable?

Actually, we believe it is none of those balance-sheet things. The biggest asset is off the balance sheet—*it's our loyal associates and our loyal customers*. Without them, a business has nothing.

Few business people, particularly the financial people, understand and act as if associates and customers are the biggest asset. When we acquired Richards, there was no doubt in our minds that the most valuable asset that we bought was the relationships that the associates had with their customers. Richards associates were huggers! But most financial people barely know what a customer is, and they certainly couldn't name many, or in some cases, any of them. Furthermore, of course, they can't figure out how to quantify their value, or measure them, since customers obviously don't appear on balance sheets. So often there is a huge disconnect between the sales/marketing side and the financial/administrative side of companies because the salespeople don't understand the economics of the business and the financial side doesn't understand the customers.

We believe the finance department and the credit department must acknowledge that associates and customers are the most important asset, and I don't mean just say it. They must know it. They must "get it." People in these departments need to actually "work" with customers. They must understand that selling expenses are necessary to build relationships that endure and bring a customer back time after time.

That's why my son Russ came up with "the Formula," a crystal-clear way for everyone to understand how hugging and making money intersect.

One day, maybe ten years ago, I was having a heavy discussion with Russ, at the time our analytical chief financial officer, about why we needed a better budget plan in order to run what was then about a $15 million business. And he said, "Dad, no, we don't need to spend hours working up budgets, financial plans, and line items. All we need is the Formula. It's very simple."

Ever since, I've called what he outlined for me that day on my white erase board the Russ Mitchell Formula. It concisely expresses the priorities when it comes to driving sales, margins, and expenses. But it comes as a function of hugging and adhering to the Formula.

The Formula ensures that we make money at what we do. It's not a retail formula or a family business formula. I believe it will work for any business, big or small, public or private, whose mindset is hugging, the passionate pursuit of relationships. Not all companies will change to a hugging culture, but perhaps the leaders of, let's say, a doctor's practice or a publishing company or an attorney's office might pick up one or two ideas here and apply it to their economic formula, which would make them more profitable.

The Formula, as Russ spelled it out to me, has just five ingredients:

1. **Drive the top line.** This means you invest everything that you can in driving sales. For us, that obviously starts with hiring great people, especially great sellers who understand hugging and relationship selling. And then you must invest in them—time, energy, and money. Hug them. They will learn and grow, and when they do, they will produce. We like to say, "Try to calculate your R.O.A., or return on assets, of your people." You can't really do it, because it's an immeasurable amount. But by trying to measure it, you keep yourself always focused on your associates. So don't begrudge paying them very well—feel great about it. I'm delighted to pay every penny to our great sellers, and especially the superstar sellers, and of course the great buyers and the great shippers and receivers, because they're worth every penny, these huggers. They are high producing and have bought into our hugging relationship culture.

    We also invest constantly in other things that drive the top line, like events, personalized letters, taking pictures of outfits, the whole repertoire of things I've mentioned that we do to please our customers. It's not just sellers, it's everyone focusing all their energy on the selling process.

2. **Achieve among the highest industry-leading margins.** Since our fundamental principle is *not to charge our customers a dollar more* than any other legitimate upper-end retailer, the secret of maximizing our margins is not only to sell more clothes at regular price than our competitors, but also to buy the best merchandise at the best price at the right time. Our mindset is about selling customers fashionable clothing—the very best we can find—and about serving them with passion beyond their expectations so they come back again and again. Notice that our mindset is not about a sale or a bargain. So when you have this mindset, you extend the hugging and the relationships to your vendors. We're not like other stores that always demand markdown money and return privileges, because so much of their business is done on sale.

We focus on key resources and invest with them. We have consolidated our base of vendors. By giving them a higher percentage of our total open-to-buy dollars, we have built an even more powerful hugging partnership.

One standard is that at least 70 percent of a particular type of merchandise must be sold before we put the remainder on sale, and most times we achieve better than that. And so we don't need to mark down items as much as some of our big-city competitors.

3. **If it doesn't touch the customer, don't spend it.** For a long time, Russell was known as "Dr. No" by our family, our senior

management, and our peers, because it seemed as if every time someone asked him about spending money on something, his answer would be a simple, unequivocal no. After a while, we finally got it, and realized that Russ was a "financial genius." What he understood and taught the rest of us was that nothing should be spent that doesn't somehow touch the customer. You won't see any money being spent in our business because of an ego trip or some grand experiment. We don't have gala family parties with camels and marching bands. We don't have fat expense accounts. We're like Sam Walton. We don't travel first class. We don't take a limousine.

Some might call us cheap, but it's a mentality that has served us well. We would rather give a bonus or a raise or some other surprise to our great people than fritter away money on an extravagance. I think our associates, vendors, and bankers like that about us.

When we say spend only when it touches the customer, hiring a great seller certainly qualifies. So do incentives to attract new customers. When we're prospecting new customers who have moved into town, we may offer them an introductory 25 percent off any single item (our most expensive item or our least expensive one), or a $100 gift certificate. It's their choice.

Here's a story I heard about a loyal Acura customer. He brought his car in to have a faulty air conditioner motor replaced. The car was eight months beyond its warranty. But the dealer saw from the maintenance records that the problem had been developing for some time. And he also knew that the customer had bought five cars from him to date. So he absorbed the cost and didn't charge anything, because he recognized that he was touching the customer and furthering the relationship with him.

Spending money where it touches the customer also means not being cheap or short-sighted when it comes to returns. Customer service people don't always realize that it costs you money to accept returns, but it's worth it in strengthening customer loyalty. Some businesses set up all sorts of obstacles to making a return, and then print them in obscure language on the back of the receipt, usually in type so small you need a high-powered microscope to read it. At Mitchells or Richards, it's easy to return merchandise.

I remember one busy afternoon ten days after Christmas. I was wandering the floor, checking things out. Out of nowhere came this loud, piercing voice: "Are you a Mitchell?" I looked up and saw this XXL man with a furrowed brow, seeming none too happy. I had to wonder if he was about to hit me. I calmly said, "Yes, sir, my name is Jack Mitchell." He said, his voice still loud, "Well, I live in New Canaan and you know what you did? You sold my daughter three Zegna shirts, and they were really expensive shirts." I nodded and said, "Yes sir, Zegna is a fine manufacturer. Highest quality, latest fashion." He continued, "Listen, you sold them in a Large, and you can plainly see that I am an Extra Extra Large." He gestured at his XXL body and smiled. "Yes, sir, I can see that," I said, realizing that he wasn't truly angry. The customers and associates who were gathered around us smiled.

"You know what just happened now?" the man said, and he put his finger right in my face. "I tried to exchange these shirts for an Extra Extra Large, and you don't have any. And your pretty girl at the customer service desk, you know what she did?" I said, "No, what did she do?" And he said, "She gave me my money back. And what's more, she did it with a smile, and Jack, there isn't a store in the world that would give me my money back on these very expensive shirts and do it with a smile!" Then he gave me a big firm handshake. Everyone around us clapped. That was an enormous hug that we got in return for giving him a hug.

4. **Carry over zero inventory from season to season.** I dream about having a business that doesn't have inventory. But retail requires it, and so we have to deal with it. At the end of a selling season, we sell every single piece of leftover inventory to wonderful retailers that are price driven, like Filene's Basement. What's so great about that? Well, although we end up taking a huge economic hit, it's something we can plan for. And then, in one day, all of the old merchandise vanishes. In its place comes fresh, new fashionable merchandise, crying to be bought.

Back in the late 1980s and early 1990s, before we established the Russ Mitchell Formula, we had so much excess inventory that we attached a big sale tent to our store, and then, like Barneys, we rented a warehouse and would hold a big warehouse sale during which we sold thousands of suits. They were mostly ones we owned, but some of them we bought from our vendor friends. After a couple of seasons, Russell and Bob said this is off Formula. They told me we were wasting too much time and energy on something that wasn't our business, rather than focusing on hugging and the Formula. That's when we added Filene's Basement to our Formula.

5. **Own your own real estate.** We've been blessed with a choice in our business over whether to own or not own our real estate. We debated long and hard within our family and within our advisory board about what route to take. The rent or occupancy costs are a huge part of the Formula. We own our own real estate. The decision to do this, on one level, was purely financial. But the most important thing, as far as I'm concerned, is that once the deal was made it allowed us to focus on our core business of hugging customers and driving the sales without having to worry about a cloud over our heads—some big landlord or real estate company raising our rent, which has happened to so many businesses. It's much easier to sleep at night. We own our territory. The territorial instinct takes over in me. It feels better. Plus, we wake up one morning ten years later and—for us at least—like our homes, the real estate has appreciated and there is lots of equity in the property.

When you have a Formula and adhere to it, you know that you're spending money only in the places where it makes sense to spend it.

Chapter 44

Cash Is King

Because of our sophisticated technology, all of the managers in the business have instant access to almost all of the details of the Formula. So it's easy for me to see what's being spent or not spent, or for Russell or Bob to see what's on order or what not to order, and what the margins are for every order. I've always loved looking at the numbers, memorizing the day's business, the margins, the cash in the bank, just like I knew the batting averages of Mantle, DiMaggio, Hank Bauer, and Gene Woodling, and how many games behind or in front the Yankees were. People who don't know me may think I'm just about numbers, but I'm not. It's just that by knowing the numbers it helps me focus my hugs.

Over my first cup of coffee at home in the morning, I always review the report that shows all individual sales the previous day of more than $2,000—by customer, sales associate, and vendor. Over my second cup of coffee, I'll often look over a report showing how our sales and markdowns are running so far that month compared to the same period a year ago. That data reinforces another key principle: Cash Is King.

Boy, do we ever believe in that. In the early days, when Dad didn't keep the closest eye on the cash flow, I discovered that we had run up $60,000 in bills that hadn't been paid, and Dad and Mom had to refinance their house to cover them. We don't ever want something like that to happen again.

Fifteen years ago, we were borrowing a fair amount of money. In 1988, we got the permits to expand the Westport store, and then the recession hit. I still wanted to go ahead with the renovations. It was a defining moment when the outside advisors on our advisory board unanimously told me that we ought to have $500,000 in the bank before borrowing the money for the expansion. At the time, we owed the banks between $1 million and $1.5 million. Wow, did that clear my sinuses.

Then Bob Matura, one of our all-time great family advisors, looked me in the eye and said, "Jack, cash is king. With money, you make honey." I got the message. It instantly became part of our culture.

I got up the next morning and began to plan to reduce our inventories, clean up our receivables, and watch our expenses. We were preparing for the days of the Russ Mitchell Formula. Before our eyes, we watched our debt evaporate.

Since then, our primary financial principle has remained Cash Is King. The trick is to stick to that idea in good times so you're able to weather the bad. Our strategy is to be conservative while still remaining open to big, bold moves when they make sense.

Years ago, Bill and I attended a meeting of fellow store owners from around the country at a small ranch outside of Tucson. I remember this great retailer from Texas who turned to me and said, "If I only hadn't wasted away all the profits and the cash that the business made when oil was king." He had tears in his eyes, because now that the oil money had dried up, he was running out of cash fast. The business survived, thank goodness, but they went through real challenging times.

I vowed to myself then that when we accumulated cash, we would invest in the business. Cash Is King, because I never want to go through the personal and professional stress and turmoil of my friend from Texas.

Chapter 45

Flowers from the Bean Counter, Flowers to the Bill Collector

For the Formula to work, everyone in your business has to not only understand it, but they also have to live it and breathe it. It must become an ingrained part of the culture. Everyone must understand when it's appropriate to spend money, and when it isn't, and that especially includes the bean counters, the people who are allergic to spending money.

I'll tell you a perfect story that points out what it means for everyone to live the Formula.

A few months after we opened the new Richards store, there was an exceedingly busy Saturday, and Todd Bonner, our controller, pitched in and agreed to help on the floor. That is what happens in a customer-centric organization. And, of course, on Game Day everyone sells. The shoe department was packed, and so Todd reported there and helped Bruce Kelly, our shoe manager, sell shoes. He quickly succeeded in helping to sell a gentleman seven pairs of Edward Green shoes. That's a very nice sale. Those shoes go for $550 to $750 a pop.

Later on, Todd came up to me and said, "Jack, I think we should send the man's wife some flowers, because she was the one that was really urging us to bring out more and more pairs for her husband to try." And I thought to myself, "What controller wants to spend money that doesn't have to be spent?" But he was with the Formula. He got it. He understood that spending a hundred dollars on orchids would touch the customer, and so it must be spent. An investment.

And that wasn't the last time he did something like that.

Another story: Helene Cote is our credit manager, and not many people feel warmly toward credit managers. When they call, that means you owe money you might not have. Helene, however, prides herself on hugging customers that haven't paid their bills. Her secret is, she's fair. If someone is honest with her, she'll give the person a lot of leeway.

People go bankrupt and run into severe financial difficulties no matter how much money they have. We had one customer who ran into very tough times and was way past due on an enormous bill to us. Rather than insist on being paid or nagging him as many bill collectors do, she would merely call him from time to time and cheerfully inquire about how he was doing and how his family was holding up. He couldn't understand why she was being so nice to him.

Helene politely worked out a payment plan over a five-year period that he was able to meet. In fact, when he was finally back on his feet, we were the first bill he paid in full. He was eternally grateful to Helene for being so understanding, and told her, "Helene, you took the time to understand the problem and believed in me, and I deeply appreciated your sensitivity and caring during the period and will always be indebted to you. You catch more flies with honey than vinegar."

And he wanted to eternally express that appreciation by making a point of sending her a beautiful bouquet of flowers for Christmas. It was during the Christmas holidays that he paid off his final installment to us.

When everyone breathes the Formula, it's clear to the entire organization what the proper use of your money is, and even the bean counters will have a reawakening.

Chapter 46

Integrity above All Else

I've said it before, but I can't stress it enough: Integrity must encompass every fiber of how you operate, and that's especially true when it comes to finances. I truly believe that by developing a hugging culture, where everyone is cared for and treated like family, you're unlikely to have the sort of shenanigans that went on at Enron and WorldCom, among other places. Like any honest businessman trying to make an honest buck, I was shocked by what transpired at those companies and feel for all the people who were hurt and betrayed by the greed of a few.

Well, without sounding presumptuous, we are proud that our culture is a far cry from those places. Years ago, we had a major theft committed by our cleaning service. We put in a claim with our insurance company, and they sent over accountants to investigate the claim, because well over $100,000 worth of merchandise had been stolen, which was really big bucks for us back when it happened. They spent days poring over our records, and finally the head honcho turned to me and said, "You really don't have another set of books, do you?" And I said, "Of course not." And what he said, which was so appalling, was, "Many small retailers do."

Well, we collected every dime of that claim. We have one set of books—honest books. Every ingredient of the Formula demands nothing less.

HUGGING STUDY GUIDE #6

Hugging produces positive financial benefits—you attract the best sellers and team members to support them, traditional marketing costs are lower, gross margins are higher, the revenue stream is long term and not highly variable, and real estate costs are lower.

Have a formula—analyze your own economic formula and analyze the economic discipline that tells everyone how hugging and making money intersect, and the cornerstone must be that you only spend money if it touches the customer.

Cash is king—you must stick to this belief in good times so you can weather the bad times and be able to reinvest in the business.

Everyone must breathe "the Formula" for it to work—and that particularly goes for the bean counters.

Integrity must encompass everything you do—this especially applies to finances, and is more important than ever.

PART SEVEN

We Love Mistakes

What to Do When You Mess Up

Chapter 47

Challenges, not Problems

In any business, things do go wrong from time to time. They have to, because you're dealing with human beings. And that's when most businesses switch to their defensive mode. How do we cover it up? How do we shift the blame? How do we pretend it never happened?

We think that's the time to really show your stuff.

We never look on mistakes as *problems*, but rather as *challenges* and *opportunities*. We recognize that tremendous bonding can occur when you recover from a mistake and go beyond a customer's expectations. That's why, when we do trip up, we try extra hard to make things right.

Indeed, some of our most memorable stories are about recovering from mistakes. Here again is why hugging is so important. The stronger the relationship you have with a customer, the easier it is to recover. Relationships, after all, encourage open and frank communication, not to mention forgiveness.

Here's a blooper we laugh about to this day. A good customer had a business meeting coming up where he wanted to look his best, and so he bought a beautiful Oxxford suit from us. It's virtually unheard of for us to send any clothing to an outside tailor shop. We lose control that way, and we don't like to lose control. But we had a big sale going on, and we were swamped with business. All the suit needed was the pant bottoms to be done. How could anyone mess that up?

Tailors almost always mark the bottoms with a chalk mark to signify where they should be finished. In a very rare instance, the tailor will want to show the customer how the pants will hang, and so he'll put a pin in at the knee to raise the bottom, and then mark it there with a chalk mark. Then he'll remove the pin. In this case, that's what our tailor did, and then the pants went out.

Who knew what the other tailor shop was thinking, but they saw the chalk marks at the knee and cuffed the pants there. They produced a pair of Bermuda shorts. The suit arrived back at our store and it went out to the customer without us noticing. He sure noticed. Fortunately, we had a great relationship with him and he had a good sense of humor. When he called us to point out the problem, Bill recalls, "He was screaming and laughing at the same time." Bill apologized profusely and told him to come in as soon as he could and we'd have a new suit ready for him that day.

Since that little episode, we've never sent any alterations out of the store. We decided we're not going to risk losing control ever again. And because of how we handled the mistake, that customer told all his friends the story of his Bermuda shorts and about how quickly we made amends.

When you do something wrong, you can bet the customer remembers it. But what they'll remember most of all is what you did to make up for the mistake.

That's why at our stores we like to say, "We love mistakes." On the face of it, that sounds a little wacky, but it's true, and it's part of what a hugging culture is about. The reason is simple. First of all, no one is perfect. And, second, often only out of mistakes can heroics occur. James Joyce once described mistakes as "portals of discovery," and I like that phrase. Mistakes are sometimes the best way to learn something new, to make adjustments to enhance your service in the future. Mistakes, of course, are entirely useless if you don't learn from them. But if you do, they're extremely worthwhile.

The issue of building an organization around forthcomingness, around honesty and openness so that others can help you and learn from you is a very big deal.

Don't get me wrong. That doesn't mean we go around rooting for everyone to make a bunch of bloopers every day. But we understand that life is full of wins and losses, perfection and imperfection, the good and the bad, and you never know where you are on that spectrum if you don't go for it and try new methods, ideas, collections, people, programs, businesses. Along the way, you are bound to make mistakes. You can't win them all.

When we look over our business, for the thousands of transactions we do, each and every one of them a possibility for an error, we find we make very few mistakes. And you shouldn't if you practice and do your blocking and tackling.

So our philosophy is not that we want people to make more mistakes, but we want people to know that we don't fear mistakes the way some bosses do. We want our associates to be willing to take the three-point shot when they have the chance to and not worry that they will get benched if they miss it. Instead they will get a high five for trying it. When that sort of atmosphere exists, when people are treated as adults, they feel comfortable.

Chapter 48

The Five-Step Mistake Solver

Since you know you're going to make occasional mistakes, you ought to have a systematic approach to deal with them that everyone knows and follows. In our case, we abide by a five-step sequence that, properly carried out, should make everyone happy.

1. **Recognize it**—unless you identify it as a mistake, you're not likely to take any corrective action. Sometimes, of course, both parties recognize it, and sometimes only we recognize it.

2. **Admit it/own it**—for God's sake, don't hide it. Rather than trying to deny mistakes or push the blame on someone or something else—"Oh, it must have been the guy in shipping" or "I didn't do anything wrong, it must have been the com-

puter"—view them as valuable learning experiences. And recognize that you "own" the mistake, even if the "fault" is
elsewhere. Sometimes, with a garment, there is a defect in the
manufacturing process, or the vendor sends the wrong color.
But, guess what, we have our label on it along with Escada's
or Zegna's. People don't return the garment and expect Zegna
to resolve it. They expect Mitchells or Richards to resolve it,
or Phyllis or John to resolve it, because they have the personal
and professional relationship with the associate and the store.
Just as I expect Continental Motors to fix my car when there's
a rattle under the passenger seat, not the car manufacturer,
and I expect the waitress to fix my steak when it comes out
well done and I ordered it rare.

Years ago, my wife and I were building a swimming pool.
It was a very big deal for us at the time. We chose a local pool
company, a third-generation family business that came highly
recommended. Anyway, you know those tiles that go around
on the top of the swimming pool near the surface? Well,
I came home one day a half hour early to check on the construction of the pool, and to my eye the tiles didn't match.
The aqua blue on one tile was different from the blue on the
tile next to it. They were pretty close, all in the blue family,
but they didn't match.

I went crazy. I couldn't believe it. How could this high-
quality swimming pool company put in tiles that didn't
match? So I called up Joe Scott, the owner, who had sold me
the pool, to complain. He let me vent for a while, and then
he patiently explained how every tile was kilned separately
and therefore they would never be the same. "I don't care,"

I said. "They look awful." He said, "Jack, what's the worst that can happen? We'll come back tomorrow and rip out every one and you can come home and say, move this one here and put that one there, or we'll get the cheap tiles that really do match and put them in instead." But then he said, "Trust me, Jack, when the water gets in the pool and the light reflects back into the pool, you will never say the tiles don't match. They will look great."

Well, by saying right off that he would come over and rip out the tiles—that he owned the mistake—rather than getting defensive or making excuses, he just took the wind out of my sails. It was so easy on his part. And so I trusted him, and of course he was right. The tiles did look great once the water was in the pool.

That's how we defuse anger. Without any ifs, ands, or buts, we always say, "It's our fault. Let's see what we can do about it." That immediately calms the customer down.

3. **Apologize**—and you must act quickly. Not two or three days later, or heaven forbid, a couple of weeks later. If you wait too long, the person will have built up a grudge that will be much harder to defuse. What's more, he will have probably complained about you to his wife, his friends, the next-door neighbor, and the mailman, and they'll start telling others about it. Before you know it, your mistake is all over town. Suddenly you've got bad word of mouth circulating. If you make amends quickly, the exact opposite will happen. The person will tell others about how wonderfully you handled the situation, and a minus will turn into a plus.

4. **Fix it**—recover in a way that is hopefully a win-win situation. One time a woman bought a gown from us that she needed two days later for a very important formal affair in New York City. Beverly Martin, her sales associate and our assistant manager, said, "Don't worry, we will deliver this beautiful gown to your home by three thirty that afternoon." Bev was working the late shift the day the gown was promised to be delivered. The first thing Bev did when she came in at 1 P.M. was go to the tailor shop to check that the gown was done so she could hand it to the delivery person to make sure it was delivered on time.

Panic! She couldn't find the dress. She soon learned it had been out on the wrong rack and it had been sent via UPS to the customer's home. The delivery wasn't due until 5 P.M. A driver was picking her up to take her to the city at 4. Bev was literally in a cold sweat when I caught wind of the mistake. "It's a mistake, Bev," I said. "Let's figure out what our alternatives are. What can we do?"

We had a plan.

Bev composed herself sufficiently to go to the phone and call the customer and tell her the truth. A mistake had been made. She was sorry, and we were doing everything we could to locate the dress, but she should be prepared to wear another gown just in case.

Dan Cote, our Richards shipping associate, got on the phone to UPS, and told them this was an emergency and we had to locate the UPS delivery now, please. He was given a special phone number the public can normally never access and was told that the truck was somewhere in the middle of its route, and had quite a few stops before it would get to this woman. "Just tell me where the truck is now!" Dan pleaded.

Dan got the address of where the truck would be in fifteen minutes, and in stepped Robin Adelman, a fellow associate who had a new car with one of those fancy-dancy satellite mapping coordinate computers that tell you the fastest way to get to a specific destination. Robin dashed for her car and, moving at close to the speed of sound, found the truck. It was parked outside someone's house where the driver was delivering a package. After notifying the driver of who she was, lest he think she was some mad woman who vandalized UPS trucks, Robin climbed into the back of the truck and hurriedly searched through the slew of packages until she found the one with the dress inside. She hopped back into her car and rushed over to the customer's house, delivering the dress with minutes to spare.

And of course the customer had a big smile on her face. She was the talk of the ball, and called Bev the next day to thank her profusely for going the extra mile. Hug, hug!

5. **Give the customer a hug**—once you've fixed the mistake, don't leave it at that. Give the customer something that makes them feel that their part of the win is extra special—a personalized note, a free tie, a flower, whatever.

A friend of mine rented a car recently and returned it to a drop-off place she hadn't been to before. She had all sorts of problems figuring out where to leave the car. Once she finally got to the checkout desk, she was determined never to use that rental agency again. But not only did the clerk reassure her that they were putting in new signs to make it clear what to do, but she handed her a coupon for a free rental whenever she wanted to use it. My friend told her, "Now I can't get mad at you."

If you're serious about fixing mistakes, you must have a methodology that everyone consistently follows.

Chapter 49

Don't Punish, Just Pet It

Most of the time, we're able to use our mistake solver to make everyone happy, but even when things don't turn out so well, we never track down who was at fault and ream out the person. That's not our style. We would go back and find out why the mistake happened, and improve our systems to cut down on that type of mistake happening again. But one of our important principles is that no one gets blamed for doing something wrong. Whenever someone fouls up, whether it's something minor or major, we resolve things so nobody ends up being punished. We don't believe in punishment. I picked that up from raising our kids.

When the kids were young, we used to take them to Florida to visit my parents in Pompano Beach, and we always made a point of going to a Polynesian restaurant called Mai-Kai in Fort Lauderdale. Russell, in particular, loved that place. In 1974, when he was eleven, he got very argumentative about something. It was obviously trivial, because I can't even remember what it was. I got so mad that I told him, "OK, you can't go to Mai-Kai." He stomped off to his room and wouldn't talk to me. I'm a talker, and I'm used to talking things through, but he was insistent on avoiding me.

For some reason, I had this book on my bedside table, *P.E.T.: The Proven Program for Raising Responsible Children*, written by Dr. Thomas Gordon. It offers step-by-step advice to resolve family conflicts so that everyone feels he has won. The book basically said that you go to school to study to become a doctor or a lawyer or an Indian chief, and then you become a parent—but no one ever teaches you how to be a parent. You never get a chance to take Fatherhood 101 or Motherhood 101. The odds are you probably had some sort of love-hate relationship with your own parents. They probably used too much authority, or maybe they let you run wild. If they were too authoritarian, you try to be less authoritarian, or if they were too laissez-faire you try to be stricter. Probably you do a little of both.

The book shares skills that help you try to listen more attentively to your child and then send a strong message about how you feel about something. If you can't convince them by relating your strong message—you shouldn't drink and drive because you might crack up the car and hurt somebody or yourself—then you have a conflict, so you have to brainstorm and come up with a compromise. If you're wrong, you apologize. And rather than beating up on them, or taking the car away, or not letting them go to a restaurant, the book also says you have to find a place to negotiate, whether it's the United Nations or the living room, and come up with something that is an acceptable win/win for both parent and child.

I stayed up the entire night reading. I swallowed the concepts hook, line, and sinker. I had been wrong. I wanted to go to Mai-Kai with my son, probably more than Russell did. So I was punishing myself too. The next day, Russell went out swimming in the ocean in an inner tube, so I got a tube and paddled out to join him. I told him I had been wrong, we're going to Mai-Kai and we're going to sit down and throw out some ideas and work this out. And we did, and I told him, "I'm not going to do punishments anymore. Instead, we're gonna work things out together."

The book gave me a formula as a guideline to help me raise our children, and I took those lessons and applied them to the business. P.E.T. became a part of me, and put into a paradigm for me exactly how I felt about communication in general and conflict resolution.

So we don't try to apply punishment, but we brainstorm and work things out with associates in a consensus manner. Whenever there's a problem at the store, I say to myself, "Let's P.E.T. it."

Chapter 50

Once Is Enough

We never go crazy when we make a mistake, but I consider it a big deal if we make the same mistake twice. Loyal customers are forgiving, but we all have our limits. If someone comes in three times and something goes wrong every time, that customer is bound to take his business elsewhere.

How often have you gone to a restaurant and they don't have your reservation and the place is packed? The first time it happens, you'll probably overlook it if you really like the food and ambiance. But if it happens again, they may lose you as a customer. It's really important to me that the dry cleaner iron the sleeves on my shirts properly so they don't pucker up. My old dry cleaner couldn't seem to get how important this was to me. Even after I complained several times, the shirts still came back with puckered sleeves. So I went to another cleaner, who did it right.

I make a point of never making a "promise" to anyone, but instead I "commit." I read once that losers promise, and winners commit. The point is, you can't deliver on every promise, but when you commit to someone you're telling the person you're going to do the absolute best you can. And one thing we really commit to is not to foul up twice.

It happens now and then that we commit to having a dress ready for Tuesday night because the customer needs it that night to wear to an event. Somebody writes down to have it ready for Wednesday night. She shows up, and no dress. We apologize profusely and drop everything and do the alterations immediately and deliver it to her.

Normally, if there's a good relationship, the customer of course forgives us. We're human, and we made it up to her. But the associate needs to make a note in that customer's profile about that mistake so extra caution is taken the next time and the time after that to see that it doesn't happen again. If we do something like that again, then the customer concludes that we're sloppy or have bad systems.

Middle initials are important to any business. Why? Because a lot of people have both the same first and last names. In our business, we easily have ten or fifteen John Smiths. In the past, we've occasionally sent the wrong merchandise to the wrong John Smith, until we made sure we got all the middle initials and paid close attention to them. John Smiths are probably constantly getting mixed up with one another wherever they do business, so you can imagine how good they're going to feel if they find a business that consistently doesn't foul up their orders. You'd be amazed at how many other duplicate names you're going to have, even in a fairly small business.

This is where technology is so important. We get those middle initials and put them in our system so we don't trip up. We have all sorts of safeguards built in, and we constantly add to them. For billing purposes, our system won't allow you, say, to enter a tie for $5,000 or socks for $850. Automatic markdowns for menswear sale items are inserted into the computer so that if the customer service associate forgets to put the markdown in, the system automatically charges the sale price.

If you take the first mistake you make seriously, there's no excuse if you repeat it.

Chapter 51

Sometimes You Have to
Shut Things Down

When it comes to business ideas, you can't be too proud and you can't be stubborn. If something really isn't panning out, there's only one way to fix it—shut it down, and fast. And again, instead of beating yourself up, learn something from what you did.

Probably the biggest business-idea mistake I ever made was the creation of a separate company back in 1989 or 1990 called Corporate Clothing Services. It started with a simple observation. Clearly, during the eighties we sold a lot of men's suits (plus blue blazers with gray pants). Probably 25 to 35 percent of our business in suits was done in four different colors: blue, gray, blue striped, and gray striped. A fifth, maybe, was a basic Prince of Wales glen plaid. They were different fabrics, different qualities, different prices, but four or five suits were the backbone of our business. If you walked into any corporate headquarters or office in Connecticut or New York, 80 percent of the men and even many of the women (remember those silly floppy bows on women?) had on this "uniform." Indeed, John T. Molloy made lots of money writing a book called *Dress for Success*, which recommended this uniform.

In addition to this simple observation, I got a call from a senior vice president of Pitney Bowes named Peter Fairbough. Pitney Bowes makes those postage machines that you and I use to put stamps on mail, and its corporate headquarters was in Stamford, Connecticut. Now, Peter knew the importance of the first impression given when wearing the corporate uniform. And so he came to me with a challenge: He had 7,000 to 10,000 "servicemen," who every day went out to General Motors and Mitchells/Richards and other businesses to fix their mailing machines when they broke down. The challenge was, they didn't look like they could fix the machines. They were servicemen wearing sloppy clothes, as opposed to a Xerox or IBM customer service associate, who wore a blue suit, white shirt, and tie when they came to fix a company's copy machine or computer.

Peter tried a simple experiment: He gave suits to all the servicemen in one office in Dallas, while everyone in another office in Dallas continued to wear the same sloppy clothing. The companies raved about the service they got from the suit guys, even though they didn't always fix the machines perfectly the first time. Somehow the companies thought they had fixed the machines. The Pitney Bowes office got feedback like, "It's great that this man came and fixed the machine, and then I guess it must have broken down three or four hours later." You get the point: Clothes enhance the professional image and even make you think good things happened that didn't.

After that little experiment, Pete asked me to do a seminar for district managers in Kansas City to talk about what I now call The

Business of Dress^{SM}. I stressed how important clothing is to making first impressions.

When I finished, I sat down to dinner with eight district managers of Pitney Bowes. And they all said, "Where can we buy these types of suits?" I said, "Well, where do you live?" One lived in Pittsburgh, so I told him Larrimor's. Someone else was in Seattle, and I told him why not Mario's. Anyway, you get the point. They had no idea where to go. Who to trust. They asked me, "Can you come to our offices, can you do a corporate catalogue?"

Well, I came back to the store, and within a year we had a whole company set up to call on the corporate offices in Fairfield County, Connecticut, and dress their employees. I thought we were going to go like gangbusters. We actually took office space in Norwalk. We built fixtures to hold suits and sport coats, and assigned a seasoned sales associate to the office.

For all our good intentions, it was a big flop. A major mistake. Within a year we closed it, and lost a lot of money. More important, we lost focus. It took a lot of my time. I firmly believed we could do a lot of business, but I was wrong.

But of course I learned a lot. We didn't get the orders, because top American leaders did not want to tell their executives what to wear. They felt it was fine to have guidelines on what was appropriate dress, but it was not fine to impose a mandate on exactly what everyone had to wear. That was just taking things a little too far. And I never could have learned this, if I hadn't tried the field goal from the 50-yard line.

But the most important thing I learned was that when something doesn't work, don't prolong the agony. The best way to deal with the blunder is to cut your losses.

Chapter 52

How Are We Doing?

A mistake that occurs that the customer knows about but you don't is the most challenging of all, because if you don't know about it, obviously, you can't do anything about it. So you really have to encourage your customers to share their annoyances when they occur and not remain silent or not return.

One time a gentleman came in and he had gained a lot of weight since his last visit to the store. He was examining a jacket and the associate helping him shook his head and said, "I don't think that pattern would look good on you." It wasn't meant to be insulting, but it was clear to the customer what he meant: That pattern wouldn't look good on someone who is fat. The man was annoyed, and he abruptly stopped coming in. Finally, wondering what was up, Bill went over to his house and in his inimitable way patched things up. But if we hadn't been proactive and gone and asked the customer, we would have lost him to our competition.

All the time, we make it clear to our customers that we're human and make mistakes, but we very much want to learn from our mistakes. We don't want to simply hear praise from our customers, though we certainly enjoy it as much as anyone. We want to know things they don't like, so we can improve. If they don't tell us we're doing something wrong, how are we going to fix it?

That's why we ask our customers, over and over, how are we doing? And we listen through independent outside ears. For well over fifteen years, we have used focus groups and telephone surveys. We have found most recently that the written survey gets much better, open, and honest information, especially since we are using a very professional research firm.

We send out surveys between two and four times a year. The last survey we did showed that 94 percent of our customers were extremely or very satisfied with their shopping experience, up from 91 percent in the previous period. Bob Shullman, president of Shullman Research Group, told us, "I've never seen numbers that high, even with the private banking clients I've worked with."

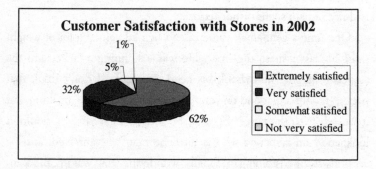

Customer Satisfaction with Stores in 2002

- ■ Extremely satisfied
- ■ Very satisfied
- □ Somewhat satisfied
- □ Not very satisfied

1%
5%
32%
62%

That feedback from someone who has conducted over 2000 customer feedback surveys for all types of industries makes us enormously pleased, and also motivates us to get to 95 or 96 the next time. Actually, my vision is to hit 100 percent, and we are consistently striving to get there.

At the bottom of a survey, we always give the customer the option of identifying themselves. We like to know the person's name, especially if they're complaining about something, because then we'll go out of our way to specifically address the issue.

One of the nice benefits of relationships is that customers don't just toss your surveys in the trash with the junk mail. As an extra hug, though, we send a gift certificate to anyone who completes the survey. This encourages them to take the time to sit down, think about the questions, and then make the check marks and write lots of comments. They want to help us, they care about us, and they want us to be better. And so do we. They know we will listen. And we do.

To top it off, many of those we survey do use the gift certificates to come visit us and make some purchases. So the survey winds up being a revenue generator.

But the most common way we get feedback is by asking customers on the selling floor while we're serving them. Because we have personal relationships with our customers, they are comfortable being blunt with us and know they won't hurt our feelings.

And customers frequently write to us when something's on their mind. Just the other day, a woman complained that the hot-water dispenser in our hospitality area was potentially dangerous. I immediately e-mailed her back to apologize and told her we'd fix the spout. And that's what we did. We got a new hot-water dispenser that is easier and safer to use.

If you're really serious about fixing mistakes, you have to ask your customers to tell you openly and honestly what bothers them. The better you cultivate personal relationships with them, the more likely they'll tell you.

HUGGING STUDY GUIDE #7

Mistakes are challenges and opportunities, not problems— out of mistakes, heroics can occur. Customers always remember when you foul up, but what they remember best of all is what you did to fix or correct it.

Follow the five-step mistake solver—recognize it, admit it/ own it, apologize, fix it, give the customer a hug.

No one is to blame—don't punish someone for making a mistake, but work out a way for it not to happen again so that everyone feels good.

Don't commit the same mistake twice—enough is enough. Track mistakes so a customer doesn't suffer the same indignity more than once.

If something doesn't work, end it—sometimes the best way to deal with a business mistake is to abandon the practice altogether.

Ask customers how you're doing—the only way to find out is to ask, so listen and learn.

PART EIGHT

The Power of New

Constantly Freshen Your Hugging Culture

Chapter 53

Having an Alive Organization

Some years ago, when my son Bob and I were on a plane crossing the Atlantic to Italy, we were analyzing our turn rates on specific products and classifications. Zeroing in on what were the fastest-turning items, we realized that four of the five top ones were either new lines or a new product in an existing line. It got us thinking, and Bob articulated what was going through my mind when he said, "You know, Dad, we need to always have something new. It's the Power of New."

It's true. Customers are constantly searching for something new. There are always the core products—basics, we call them—that sell steadily, year after year, and that you can't be without. But they're not enough to sustain a growing business. People want that thrill, that buzz of the new.

Now, that seems pretty obvious when you're in the fashion clothing business. We always need something new to feature to get our loyal customers into the store at the beginning of the season. But it goes far beyond a new look from Tommy Bahama or a powerful new line like Armani Black Label for women.

We apply it to everything we do, whether it's hiring a great new associate, coming up with a new way of profiling customers, or adding a new technique to the Play Book. Because we've recognized the Power of New.

It's an incredibly potent force, a way of stimulating and invigorating your business, and it's indispensable in the highly competitive world we live in. A business must have new ideas and new ways of doing things. Without new ideas—new ways to hug, new ways to get closer to the customer, new ways to get into their heads and their closets—a business quite simply has no future.

One way we like to express it is, "The best hugs are given by winners, and winners must continue to innovate." There's no denying that hugs can get stale if they're always the same. They lose their effectiveness. Bill Parcells, coach of the championship New York Giants football team, always had a new spread or trick play or two designed to score. His players and his fans learned to accept the surprise, the unexpected, the new, which helped create energy and enthusiasm, and when the team executed the play perfectly, it was a super *wow*!

Believing in the Power of New creates a vibrant spirit, an environment of listening and learning, and it produces what I think of as an *alive* organization. I've always loved a biological model for business, and so we all know that an organism either grows or it dies. There's no in-between. It's the same for an organization. If you stop learning, you'll die.

One way you grow is by always being on the lookout for new people. In the section on hiring and caring for great associates, I made it clear how important great people are to the business. But most businesses only hire when they have an opening or are expanding. Even if we're at full staff, even if times are lean, I'm always receptive to a great seller who has the qualities that we look for. It's a principle I learned a long time ago, crystallized by a story an old man told me in the back of a bus in China, of all places. It's too long a story to get into, but his point was that life is like a merry-go-round, and you have to be prepared to see the brass ring and act accordingly to grab it. It may not be the best time, but if you don't grab it when you see it, that particular opportunity will pass you by forever.

We know that when you add great new people, you add tremendous synergy to the team. They not only play with their teammates, but they inspire them to new heights. Think of when Jason Giambi came to the Yankees.

There are so many examples I could offer in our business, but the one that I will never forget is how we hired Phyllis Bershaw, who turned out to be a Hall of Fame hugger.

It happened back in June 1990. I was at home, doing something I don't do very often, which was resting. I had fallen asleep in a lounge chair by the pool. The telephone woke me up. It was a wonderful old friend who had worked for us years ago. She went into this long song and dance about this amazing seller named Phyllis Bershaw. "She's the best I've ever seen," she said, and a recommendation like that gets my attention fast.

This happened to be the height of the recession, and the last thing any business was doing was hiring anyone. But believing in the Power of New, I didn't hesitate a second. I looked up her number, called her, and soon she was part of our team. What Phyllis brought was not only hundreds of new customers and clients of her own, but also a new level of excellence and expertise that sellers in Westport had never seen before. For instance, Phyllis quickly demonstrated that she could call up a friend and client and within a half hour that client would be coming through the door asking Phyllis what product was so new that she couldn't wait until the next day to buy it.

It's the same way with product. When you bring in something new—the right something new—it energizes the whole store. We added women's Prada shoes in Mitchells. We began with a small, but meaningful selection. Overnight, it became the leading shoe brand in the store, and gave the store a new cachet. When we expanded Mitchells in 1992, we added a whole new designer department of women's clothing, and our women's business exploded. It was similar at Richards when we started a women's business.

It's the Power of New. Another opening, another show.

What you must recognize is that it's just not enough to be the best. While it's a wonderful feeling and we are proud of it in our market area, we have to constantly think of new ways to remain dominant.

A friend of mine has had a mortgage with the same bank for years, and the only communication he has ever received from them is his monthly mortgage coupon. Just before Christmas, the mail came and there was what looked like a Christmas card from the bank. He thought that was pleasant of them, but since he wasn't much interested in sterile, corporate cards, he was going to throw it away without even opening it. But out of curiosity, he tore it open anyway. It was in fact a card, but included with it was a 30-minute prepaid phone card as a present so he could call out-of-town friends or relatives during the holidays.

He was floored. That's what the Power of New does.

Chapter 54

Don't Be Handicapped by Experience

It's often easier for new people to see things in fresh ways and understand the Power of New. But since your core staff is comprised of well-tenured associates, you have to constantly challenge them so they will think differently. We remind them, "Sometimes you can be handicapped by experience."

Frequently it is very difficult to change a mindset if you have been doing something one way for a long time. Another way to look at it is that you have to think *outside* the box while working *in* the box. Don't stop doing all the wonderful things that have gotten you where you are, the tried-and-true systems that have been proven to work; but also be open to the Power of New and be willing to listen, learn, and grow.

The Power of New can come in the form of something as subtle as changing a single word in your goals. It occurred to me about ten years ago that "satisfied" customers were not good enough and we needed to cultivate "very" satisfied customers. That really helped differentiate us in the way we looked at customers, because we developed the attitude that you needed to go beyond the customer's satisfaction every visit.

In the last couple of years, we have evolved to where we have three degrees of satisfaction that we measure in our customer surveys: somewhat satisfied, very satisfied, and a new top tier of extremely satisfied. This might sound like splitting hairs, but when we survey customers, we actually find that those who describe themselves as extremely satisfied rather than very satisfied are more loyal and do more of their shopping with us. So our associates work harder now at profiling the customers and clients. We look at the hugs we do, and do even more of them.

Two industries I've long felt have been handicapped by experience are the health-care and fast-food industries. Their customer service just never seems to change. When I go to a hospital or doctor, I so often feel like a number. Unless you really know the doctor, just getting test results is such an ordeal. They come in the mail two or three weeks later, and when you try to reach the doctor to discuss them he's at a convention in Belgium. Why couldn't test results be e-mailed, and why couldn't the doctor include in the e-mail two or three specific times he would be free to discuss the results? I've always thought it would be great if McDonald's or Burger King had "greeters" at the door to welcome customers. I know that goes against the thinking in that business, but that's exactly why I think it would be so refreshing.

Here's an example in our business. It's a common mindset in sales to wait for customers to come to you, to do your selling in the store. But we've increasingly been pushing the idea of associates visiting customers on their turf; we've even set performance goals related to how often our sales associates are out of the store seeing customers in their homes and offices.

One way we increasingly do this is through a concept known as "closet cleans." A customer might say to an associate, "Gee, I have to check my closet to see if I have that color blue," and that gives the associate the opportunity to respond, "You know, I would be delighted to come take a look at your closet." If the customer agrees, the sales associate makes an appointment, visits the customer's home, and goes through the entire closet or, in some cases, closets.

We literally go into their bedrooms, by invitation of course, and we clean their closets. Because everyone is very busy and their expertise is not clothing, we give advice. This you should throw out, this you should give to Goodwill, this you can alter a little bit, this you can mix and match this way. We actually take pictures for them of their various combinations for their own reference.

That way, you see what exists in the closet and what needs tweaking—a slight alteration or updating—what's ready for discarding, and where there are holes. And you learn.

While you're doing the clean, you talk to the customers. What's the next event on their schedule? Oh, they're going to the opera. Do they have something to wear? No, not really. Well, a beautiful beige suit just came in, and I see you don't have that color.

This is very important in building a relationship. A woman who has let you into her bedroom to look at her clothes has to trust you. You've taken the time to learn about her lifestyle, and she appreciates that. And it helps us become more efficient. We see what our customers have. We take an inventory. So if a fabulous navy outfit comes in, we won't call someone when we know she has that in her closet. Or we can resuscitate things. We see a dress. Have you thought about putting that together with this shawl you have? You're not making a sale, just offering some expert advice. Then they see that you're not there just to sell to them but to offer service to them.

Interestingly, we find that men are more open to us cleaning their closets than women, because women feel more sure of themselves. But once even a self-assured woman allows us in, she finds we can offer a lot of useful advice.

Naturally, we're looking to sell by pointing out deficiencies and gaps, and in some cases there's an instant payoff. Jeff did a closet clean recently where the man needed only one suit, but he was really lacking in casual clothing. Jeff asked him if he wanted to come in and get some things to fill the void. He came in that afternoon and bought about $8,000 worth of clothing.

Other times, it's building for the future. One associate spent a morning doing a closet clean and complained that the customer bought only two pairs of khakis. We pointed out that he was being short-sighted. Performing that service increased the level of trust and will certainly make that customer even more loyal.

It can be a little challenging to offer closet cleans because some customers get a bit suspicious. What do they want to look at my closet for? We've found that the best time to ask is when someone is moving and has to go through their closets anyway or when someone's size has changed. They're looking for help then.

So if you're not handicapped by experience, your eyes will open to new opportunities you never thought possible.

Chapter 55

Share Your Best Ideas

One very important source of innovation for us is by learning from others in our business, and we do that by sharing with them, and I mean sharing everything, from how we do things to what our financials are like. We participate in two valuable organizations. One is the Men's Apparel Forum Group, which consists of a collection of family-owned stores that are located in different cities around the country and thus don't compete with each other. We meet twice a year and swap ideas that each of us has tried and found works. And one of the most powerful things we learn is what not to do, because someone has tried something and it didn't work.

It's a win-win situation for all of us. The other organization is the IMG, or International Menswear Group, which consists of stores in other countries. We do the same thing with them.

The ideas that come from sharing with similar businesses can be indispensable. From a store called Kaps in the Boston area, for instance, we learned of an inventory-control company that we hired to help us get our hands around our out-of-control inventory problem during the 1990–91 recession. Plus, Kaps helped us establish our relationship with Filene's Basement, and that has become an important concept for us and part of our Russ Formula.

Members also pick up valuable ideas from us that boost their business. Erla and Saevar, who run a fabulous clothing store in Iceland, have adopted a host of our concepts, including thank-you notes and personalized birthday gifts for their customers. They serve Italian coffee and other refreshments to everyone, even sometimes going out on the street and offering them to passersby. For the last three years, they've had live concerts in their store and recorded a CD that they send out to their top three thousand customers as a Christmas gift. On the cover of the last one, they put a beautiful picture of their family, as we like to do in some of our mailings.

Here's an idea I shared with the Forum Group. Years ago, I was walking around the Hickey-Freeman factory and I noticed all these small bolts of fabulous fabrics stacked on the shelves. Known as "ends," they're the leftovers from making suits. Sometimes Hickey-Freeman makes them up into suits and sends them to its outlet stores. So I said, why don't we buy them, at a reduced price of course, wrap them up in boxes, send them to our best customers, and say, "If you'd like a suit made of this fabric, we'll sell it to you for six hundred dollars instead of nine hundred." We tried it with fifty customers and ten gentlemen loved the fabrics and are now wearing new suits. A hug for all. Recently, we decided to revive the idea and do it again.

Any industry could do what we do in the Forum Group and IMG. Hardware stores could get together. Health-care providers could get together. Funeral parlors could get together. A lot of them do at trade association conventions, but those are often large, unwieldy meetings that happen once a year. Until businesses intimately share everything about themselves and how they care for their customers in small groups, they're not going to benefit fully from the Power of New.

Chapter 56

What about 2015?

I'll bet it was about seven or eight years ago when I learned that several members of our sales force were frustrated with me. "You're always sending mixed messages," one of them said. "On the one hand, you say we are the best sellers in the world, and then in the next sentence or maybe the next day you are jumping up and down with new ideas and saying we need to improve because you would like us to do this or do that."

That night, I slept on his comments, and the next day I came up with a simple bar graph to explain what I was trying to get at. A lot of businesses use the expression "raising the bar," and so do we, but we don't just use the expression, we actually act on it. We believe you have to raise the hugging bar every year or you'll slip.

And I demonstrated just that on the bar graph: If you rank a perfect 10 in service in 1995, meaning you're the best you can be, that 10 will equate to a 5 in 2002 and probably a 3 in 2015, because everyone else is innovating and improving. If you keep on doing everything the same way, before long you'll be worse—much worse. I believe we have the best sales associates and best buyers and best of just about everything. For today. What about 2004? What about 2005? We may be a 9 or 10 in 2000, but if we close our eyes, we could be a 6 or 7 in 2015. If we do nothing new from 1995 on, we might become a 3 in 2015.

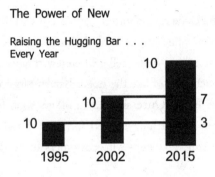

The Power of New

Raising the Hugging Bar . . .
Every Year

The *Key* to Exceeding Expectations

Now, an important part of this concept is that you don't lose the fundamentals that you learned in 1995. You build on them. And, in a sense, you take them for granted. It's the foundation that is so important. You don't stop taking packages out to the car, you do more of it. You don't stop collecting pertinent information about customers, you collect more of it. You don't stop hugging, you hug more and in new ways.

Here's a little example. Rita Roman is a remarkable sales associate who is multitalented. An individual who wants to do it all, she is very driven and always looking for ways to raise the bar. When she joined us some years ago, she wanted to become a great seller and a great menswear manager. We spent an enormous amount of time getting to know each other and building our relationship. I began using the exercises I learned from David Bork, our family business consultant, and the P.E.T. strategies with Rita. Then we introduced Michael Yacobian and the Client Accumulation Program, on how to turn customers into clients—be proactive, not reactive; focus on relationships, not transactions.

One day Rita came racing into my office and said that it all clicked for her. She got it! She became a full-fledged hugger. Rita went on to become our first million-dollar seller when few, if any, sellers in America sold that much, sort of like the Roger Banister four minute mile of upper end retail sales. Once she did it, others soon followed. They became believers. Something clicked for them when they saw Rita profiling and taking next steps with customers and turning them into clients.

Rita started selling women's as well as men's clothing, and eventually got to $2 million in sales, and then beyond. She was serving the husband and the wife. When her son was born, she didn't want to lose a beat with her customers so we set up a computer at her home while she was on maternity leave. Within several weeks, she was making appointments, and I think she kept all of her customers and clients during one of the most exciting stages of her life. Year after year, she keeps raising the bar.

Think of JetBlue, the new airline that raised the bar for the airline industry by introducing things like inflight yoga and providing an individual satellite TV for each passenger so you don't have to watch a movie you've already seen four times. A senior beverage executive

once shared with me that no matter how well his company is performing, he's always saying to his team, "What's next?"

When it comes to raising the bar, there are two fundamental principles.

1. **Everyone must raise the bar.** Raising the bar is a personal
   quest, but it needs to be corporatewide.

   As a leader, it's important not to simply tell people what
   to do. If you want everyone to raise the bar, I find it's much
   better that you tell your associates stories, and give them examples of things that could be done to help them. At times,
   I get frustrated and exasperated when I see someone not doing
   something that is so obvious to me. I do my best to let it go
   and to reinforce the correct behavior.

   It's preferable by far that our associates see someone else
   in the store doing something "heroic," and be inspired.
   They'll think, if she can do it, I can do it too. And they can.

   Norberto, one of our sales associates at Richards, didn't
   really have the confidence or feel enabled to do heroics on his
   own. But he had watched Frank and John accomplish heroics,
   and he began to muster the courage.

   A short while ago, Norberto got a call from an executive
   in Mexico, and he was desperate. He was on an airplane, coming to Greenwich with his wife and daughter for a funeral in
   the area. He thought his wife had packed his suit, and she
   hadn't. The man would be checking into his hotel that evening, and had to leave for the funeral a couple of hours before
   our store opened the next morning.

Norberto called the man's assistant in Mexico and told him to get one of the man's suits from his closet and take the measurements. Meanwhile, the man had shopped with us years before and so we had evidence of his tastes. Norberto picked out a navy suit, had it altered, and since I had a business meeting at the Greenwich Hyatt, where the man was staying, I delivered it and left a message telling him where he could reach me if there was a problem. Everything went smoothly, and when I happened to meet the man and his family a couple of days later, he couldn't have been more grateful. He said, "Norberto is my hero."

That's because Norberto raised the bar for himself.

2. **Don't raise it too fast.** Speed is very important when it comes to raising the bar. As a manager, if you move too slowly, you miss opportunities. If you move too fast, people get discouraged. They can't keep up. They think there's something wrong with them. The problem is, you raised the bar too high too soon.

When that happens, the fundamentals that are part of the bar from the previous year suffer. In other words, if you were rated a nine out of ten in calling every customer on your satisfaction list, making sure they were extremely satisfied with their shopping experience, and then you immediately tried to raise the bar by putting in a whole new program on profiling and you didn't take the time to think out the new program well enough, then probably your performance on satisfaction calls will go down to six or seven.

Superstars can handle and thrive on adding new things and

growing fast. But people develop at their own pace, so you have to be very careful and get feedback on the new programs to make sure the more established programs don't suffer. If the sales associates feel that you are just piling on more work and you haven't taken the time to prioritize or educate them enough so they can multitask in a positive way, then it's a huge slap.

So it's vital to know your associates well enough that you raise the bar the appropriate amount. One woman, a huge hugger and real relationship builder, came up for her annual review, and she was doing everything right and then some. The only part of the bar that needed to be raised for her was, she needed to wait on more people. There was no doubt in our minds that she was capable of it, she just needed a little prodding.

She spent a lot of time hugging the customers she had, and so she didn't look to acquire as many new customers as we knew she could. So we gave her the goal of adding sixty clients in the next year. We negotiated this number with her so that it was reasonable. It was well below what another top seller was selling, but we started at that figure and then gradually increased it so she didn't feel overwhelmed.

A wonderful new associate, on the other hand, was waiting on ten to twenty customers a day. That's a lot of transactions for us, double or triple what some of our veteran associates do. What it means was she was closing each sale pretty quickly, being satisfied with selling a dress without taking the time to suggest some accessories to go with it or see if another outfit might be needed for some upcoming occasion. So we asked her to try to take more time to dig in and build more of a relationship with each customer instead of closing the sale so quickly. Her average sale was $340, while the first associate I mentioned had an average of about $1,200. By seeing fewer customers, the new associate was able to actually end up selling more.

When I think about raising the bar, I love to tell the story about my friends, their beagle, and the kennel. They live in New York City and were going on vacation for a week and needed a kennel for their beagle, Missy. Someone recommended a place in New Jersey. They called it up, and it was easily an hour's drive from them, and they didn't feel like making the trip. The kennel said, "It's not a problem, we'll be happy to pick your dog up and deliver her when you get back."

They did just that. They picked Missy up and a week later returned her, freshly shampooed, exactly when they said they would. A year later, my friends used the kennel again, and when they brought Missy back, the kennel gave my friends a handful of pictures of Missy playing with other dogs, and there were captions identifying the playmates. Here was Missy playing with Rocco. Here was Missy playing with Clarence. It was a nice touch. Later, they followed that up with cards, supposedly from those playmates inquiring as to how Missy was doing.

You would have thought the kennel had done more than enough to keep my friends as loyal customers, but they didn't quit. When my friends used them a third time, they picked up and delivered Missy, furnished photos of Missy cavorting with her playmates, and when Missy arrived home she had on a nice new sweater that the kennel had put on her as a present. I can't imagine what they will do next, but it's bound to be something unexpected. Year after year, they keep raising the bar.

Every business should be like that kennel, and that's always been our mission at Mitchells/Richards. Every day, while I'm concentrating on what we have to do that day to exceed the expectations of our customers, I'm also thinking of where we should be in excellence in 2004 and 2005 and even 2015! You have to improve—every day, every week, every month—or the world will pass you by without even a wave.

The more you hug your customers, in both the time-tested ways and new ways, the more loyal they become. They will be your customers not only for today and tomorrow, but forever. The best huggers aren't just excellent at what they do. They keep getting better. They understand that there is no limit to how high the bar can be raised. The only limit is their imagination.

HUGGING STUDY GUIDE #8

You always need something new—core products and services aren't enough, customers want that buzz of the new. Hugs can get stale if they're always the same.

Don't be handicapped by experience—don't be afraid to try something new just because you've been doing something one way forever. Learn to think outside the box while working in the box.

Share your best ideas—form a group with other noncompeting businesses in your field and swap new ideas with them; everyone wins.

Raise the bar—either you raise your goals every year or you'll slip (a 10 today is an 8 next year); raising the bar must be corporatewide, and people must do it at their own pace.

Epilogue

Can You Imagine?

Every day at Mitchells/Richards we strive to grow and do even more for our customers, and every day we continue to remind ourselves of why we do what we do.

For three generations, and hopefully many more to come, the Mitchell family has been hugging customers, and they've been hugging us back.

It's not just because our associates and customers have lots more fun than at other stores, but that's part of it.

It's not just because we learn more about our customers, but that's part of it.

It's not just because, as Bill always reminds us, "It's the right thing to do," but that's part of it.

It's not just because it makes our business more successful and more profitable than others, but that's part of it.

Most of all, as I learned from Mom and Dad back when they had three suits hanging on the racks and Nani was doing the alterations, hugging is so basic a part of human relationships that to us it seems unnatural not to do it. It's natural to treat people well and surprise them with positive acts, because that's how everyone loves to be treated. It simply feels so wonderful and great. Deep down, both in mind and spirit, I fervently believe we all quest for meaningful personal relationships in every aspect of our lives. Of course we want them with our families, but we also long for them in the workplace, and too often we forget that. Heavens, most of us spend more time in the workplace than we do at home! So we hug because we love to hug and we need to hug.

There are other businesses and business leaders that are fabulous huggers, and I salute them. Look around, and when you see them, praise them. Copy them. Learn from them. The world needs more businesses that are built on passionate relationships. It would be presumptuous of me to expect that this book alone will make you a believer. But I do hope it will get you thinking and dreaming.

Dreaming comes naturally to me, and so whenever I have a spare moment I like to close my eyes and imagine the world I would love to live in. One thing I often find myself imagining is a world full of huggers, a world full of caring, considerate people who sincerely want to make their customers feel great. Maybe that sounds too idealistic, but not to me. It sounds absolutely wonderful.

In my dream world, my *New York Times* and *Wall Street Journal* are not only delivered just at the right time, but also in the perfect spot, out in our driveway at 5 A.M., and not on our roof.

In my dream world, the lawn service actually trims the trees just the way I ask them to do it, plus they take care to blow the grass cuttings out into the lawn and not into Linda's flowerbeds and through the windows into our bedroom.

In my dream world, hotels emphasize friendly, caring managers and maids more than antiques and famous art on the walls. Even the pool attendants and the locksmiths know the customers' names.

In my dream world, when I call the phone company, the insurance agent, the hospital, or the candlestick maker, a real, live voice answers. No more of that computerized Chinese menu of options which can frustrate me to tears before I'm disconnected without ever getting the person I'm trying to reach.

In my dream world, when I go to the bank or the bakery, I'm greeted by, "Hi, how's the family?" rather than the shouted "Next," and even the plumber sends me personalized thank-you notes for being given the opportunity to fix my leaky pipe.

In my dream world, whether I go to buy tires or stereo equipment or earmuffs, everybody smiles and calls me Jack.

Sound like Fantasy Island? Maybe. Maybe not.

A world of huggers—wouldn't that be fantastic? People that are no longer impersonal, cold, or rude. They have developed a passion about positive personal relationships in their businesses. Every day they treat their customers and associates like friends, just the way they want to be treated. Every day they show how much they care.

It doesn't have to be a dream. Year after year, hugging works for us. It can work for you.

So try it. Put the book down and give somebody a hug. Give them a smile. Ask them how their kids are doing. Pick up the phone and call your best customer or your most valued supplier. See if hugging works in your business. I'll bet a nickel that it does.

Remember, everyone loves a hug!

Thank you.

Lots of hugs.

Enjoy Playing the Hugging Game

HUGGING ACHIEVEMENT TEST

(H.A.T.)

Now that you've finished the book, you might want to take one last peek at the Hugging Study Guide at the end of each chapter to refresh your memory, and then I think you'll find it educational to take the following hugging test. It's not as hard as the S.A.T., so relax and enjoy the game. It could be very revealing for your business. Hopefully, it will allow you to identify what hugging principles you may already have in place, and where you've got significant gaps. Obviously, you can't change your culture overnight and maybe you will only want to use a few takeaways—a few new ideas for your business—without swallowing or endorsing the entire hugging culture. But by analyzing your answers, you can identify and then decide if and when you want to begin implementing the changes that will truly begin or enhance a hugging culture in your business. Remember, be honest! No cheating. Have fun. Go at it with a super-positive attitude and a passion to grow!

1. Make a list of at least a dozen ways you feel you hug your customers and exceed their expectations. If you can list more than twenty, you get extra credit.

_____

_____

_____

_____

2. What are three things you do every week, month, and year for each associate you work with or who reports to you that makes him or her feel special? (Do you know their names, their spouses' names, their kids' names?)

_____

_____

_____

_____

_____

3. Do you know your top one hundred customers without looking them up? List them. How often do you see them, talk with them, hug them? If you can list 250, you're on your way to the hugging hall of fame.

_____

_____

_____

_____

_____

4. Who in your organization knows these customers? Only the sales side? How about the financial end? How about the head of manufacturing, design, marketing? What about the shipping clerks?

_____

_____

_____

_____

_____

5. What is your selling floor? Your playing field? Write it down. Do you have a policy that everyone is on the "floor" where they can see, touch, and feel real, live customers? Who has to be on the floor and who doesn't?

_____

_____

_____

_____

_____

6. What are the key traits you look for when you hire someone? Are you consistent? Does everyone who hires use the same criteria?

Do you measure your associates against performance goals only? Or do you talk about and score learning and enjoyment goals?

_____

_____

_____

_____

_____

7. Is there anyone in your organization whom you already recognize as a hugger? Who is the best relationship seller on your team? Top three, five? Remember to look throughout your entire company. Are you enabling these sellers to grow? How? List the top five programs you currently use. List the top three you would like to begin this year. List the top one you would like to see five years from now.

_____

_____

_____

_____

_____

8. Do you empower your associates to come up with hugs? Do you enable them, or simply dictate to them? If you enable them, give three examples of how you've done that.

_____

_____

_____

_____

_____

9. What kind of technology do you use? Does the software focus on tracking inventory first or customers first? How much about your customers and what they've bought do you know from your systems? Can your CEO use the system? Does he or she embrace technology?

_____

_____

_____

_____

_____

10. Do you personalize your marketing, or do you generate mass mailings by computer? When was the last time you sent a note to a customer or important business partner with a handwritten message on it, signed with a real ink pen?

_____

_____

_____

_____

_____

11. Do you isolate your biggest selling days or seasons and plan, prepare, and practice for them differently? Do you have a Play Book that helps your associates call the best "plays"? What's in it? When was the last time you asked your associates if there was anything more you could do for them to increase their sales?

_____

_____

_____

_____

_____

12. How often do you really know the score, whether you're ahead or behind? Who in your organization has access to the score? How often does your top management look at the score? Do you focus only on performance goals? Do you have enjoyment and learning goals which enhance the quality of life at work and raise the bar?

_____

_____

_____

_____

_____

13. Do you give customers what they want, or what you think they want? Do you preach, or do you listen? Give an example.

_____

_____

_____

_____

_____

14. Do you have a formula that shows everyone the connection between a focus on customers and the economics of the business? What is it? How do you decide what you spend money on and what you say no to?

_____

_____

_____

_____

_____

15. List three of the most recent mistakes you made with customers and explain how you handled them. Were you satisfied with the resolution? Was your customer? How do you really know? How did you treat the associates who made the mistakes?

_____

_____

_____

_____

_____

16. What sorts of mechanisms do you have in place to get feedback from customers? List the top five. Are you happy with the results? What do you do with the information?

_____

_____

_____

_____

_____

17. Name three "new" things you've introduced in the last twelve months, whether products, services, new ways of thinking about things, or new hires. Do you feel you have an ongoing mindset of looking for new things?

_____

_____

_____

_____

18. Do you belong to any organization for businesses in your field where you swap ideas? Can you imagine a way to set one up?

_____

_____

_____

_____

_____

19. Do you have a system in place for raising the bar with your team? Give three examples of how someone in your organization has raised the bar in the last year.

_____

_____

_____

_____

20. From your previous answers, list five hugging tips that you want to implement now and tell how you are going to do it.

_____

_____

_____

_____

_____

Congratulations on completing the Hugging Achievement Test (H.A.T.)! I hope you had fun and learned something from it. I would love to hear from you . . . feedback, comments, favorite hugging stories, nominations for "World-Class Hall of Fame" huggers (people or companies) who deliver extraordinary customer service and make you feel super great! I know we will learn from you! Write us or e-mail us at the following: jackm@hugyourcustomers.com or Jack Mitchell, c/o Mitchells, 670 Post Road, Westport, CT 06880. Thank you very much.

MITCHELL/RICHARDS HUGGING TEAM

Maria Abrantes, Robin Adelman, Chiyoko Ancrum, Jim Arndt, Dieuseul Auguste, John Awdziewicz, Yuriy Ayrapetov, Judy Barker, Michael Barrett, Norberto Barroso, Victoria Batsu, Antonio Bazar, Luis Bedoya, Nora Bedoya, Dan Beliard, Phyllis Bershaw, Andrew Bessey, Joe Biondi, Todd Bonner, Allison Borowy, Judy Brooks, Tom Brown, Susie Burian, Jim Callaghan, Nasra Capar, Bob Carella, Sophia Carella, James Cash, Ray Cerritelli, Larry Chiappetta, Rosa Chuquimamani, Belinda Cole, Rejina Cole, Domenic Condoleo, Lisa Coppotelli, Louis Corello, Lucila Correa, Dan Cote, Helene Cote, Joe Cox, Vicki Cox, Matilde Cruz, Jean Debreus, Laura Dell'Aera, Jim Denino, Joe DeRosa, Joe D'Eufemia, Anne-Marie Drumgold, Aggie Dubiel, Noella Duh, Jean Evans, Dan Farrington, Cathy Fotinopoulos, Frank Gallagi, Debra Gampel, Emmanuel Garcon, David Garr, Gloria Gekas, Pat Giannitti, Tullio Giannitti, Tullio Giannitti Jr., Arlyne Goldberg, Jackie Gordon, Tony Gregorio, Angela Guitard, Margarita Gutierrez, Tanya Hartman, Eleni Hasiotis, Phuong Heitz, Claudia Henao Builes,

John Hickey III, Eric Hollo, Kristina Hook, Kristin Hulet, John Hytros, Lisa Iselin, Amy Jarman, Hedica Jaure, Rosa Lee Jones, Bill Joyce Jr., Soula Kalomenides, Bruce Kelly, Iwona Kelly, Ginger Kermian, Elli Koumbaros, Jennifer Kowal, Cathy Kozak, Jeff Kozak, Bill Kubik, Irene Kubik, Bruce Lagerfeldt, Richard Laidlaw, Lori Land, Linda Levy, Terry Lewis, Derrick Lopez, Sylvia Lundberg, Kristen Lutz, Cruz Lynch, David Lynn, Tom Maleri, Chris Malone, Beverly Martin, Paul Mendelsohn, Rocco Messina, Pamela Miles, Andrew Mitchell, Ed Mitchell, Linda Mitchell, Bob Mitchell, Russ Mitchell, Scott Mitchell, Todd Mitchell, Bill Mitchell, Carlos Morales, Laura Murphy, Manuel Naulaguari, Ronnie Nelson, Alana New, Robert Norman, Doreen Nugent, Ferdi Ocasio, Rickee Oleet, Jill Olson, Debra O'Shea, Giuseppa Paglia, Teresa Pagliuso, Bob Palazzo, Roe Palermo, Taffy Parisi, Jung-Ae Park, Trish Patch, Edgard Paulemon, Lauren Perez, Maria Petrova, Angela Pieretti, Melissa Piorkowski, Bob Potts, Heather Raftery, Rosario Ramirez, Fabio Ramirez Jr., Trish Rapoport, Stefan Rastawiecki, Anthony Renzuella, Rob Rich, Dennis Riordan, Betsy Rojas, Rita Roman, Michele Romano, Larry Rosen, Aldo Rotino, Fatima Salvador, JoAnn Salvioli, Kathleen Santaniello, Lisa Schwartz, Jennifer Seideman, Diana Serna, Gloria Serna, Luis Serna, Michael Servidio, Evelyn Shelton, Gail Sheriff, Michael Solinas, Sonia Spencer, Giovanna Stella, Mark Taylor, Peewee Teja, Flavio Tenesaca, Hoa Thai, Susie Thomas, Nhung Thikim Tran, Georgia Tsoulfas, Iren Vass, Rita Vass, Marilyn Wallack, Heidi Williams, Patrick Williams, Janet Wilson, Lauren Wilson, Stefani York.